Editor-in-Chief and Founder:
  Lyndon H. LaRouche, Jr.
Editorial Board: *Lyndon H. LaRouche, Jr. , Helga
  Zepp-LaRouche, Paul Gallagher, Tony Papert,
  Gerald Rose, Dennis Small, Jeffrey Steinberg,
  William Wertz*
Co-Editors: *Paul Gallagher, Tony Papert*
Managing Editor: *Nancy Spannaus*
Technology: *Marsha Freeman*
Books: *Katherine Notley*
Ebooks: *Richard Burden*
Graphics: *Alan Yue*
Photos: *Stuart Lewis*
Circulation Manager: *Stanley Ezrol*

INTELLIGENCE DIRECTORS
Counterintelligence: *Jeffrey Steinberg, Michele
  Steinberg*
Economics: *John Hoefle, Marcia Merry Baker,
  Paul Gallagher*
History: *Anton Chaitkin*
Ibero-America: *Dennis Small*
Russia and Eastern Europe: *Rachel Douglas*
United States: *Debra Freeman*

INTERNATIONAL BUREAUS
Bogotá: *Miriam Redondo*
Berlin: *Rainer Apel*
Copenhagen: *Tom Gillesberg*
Houston: *Harley Schlanger*
Lima: *Sara Madueño*
Melbourne: *Robert Barwick*
Mexico City: *Gerardo Castilleja Chávez*
New Delhi: *Ramtanu Maitra*
Paris: *Christine Bierre*
Stockholm: *Ulf Sandmark*
United Nations, N.Y.C.: *Leni Rubinstein*
Washington, D.C.: *William Jones*
Wiesbaden: *Göran Haglund*

ON THE WEB
e-mail: eirns@larouchepub.com
www.larouchepub.com
www.executiveintelligencereview.com
www.larouchepub.com/eiw
Webmaster: *John Sigerson*
Assistant Webmaster: *George Hollis*
Editor, Arabic-language edition: *Hussein Askary*

EIR (ISSN 0273-6314) *is published weekly
(50 issues), by EIR News Service, Inc.,
P.O. Box 17390, Washington, D.C. 20041-0390.
(703) 777-9451*

European Headquarters: E.I.R. GmbH, Postfach
Bahnstrasse 9a, D-65205, Wiesbaden, Germany
Tel: 49-611-73650
Homepage: http://www.eirna.com
e-mail: eirna@eirna.com
Director: Georg Neudecker

Montreal, Canada: 514-461-1557

Denmark: EIR - Danmark, Sankt Knuds Vej 11,
basement left, DK-1903 Frederiksberg, Denmark.
Tel.: +45 35 43 60 40, Fax: +45 35 43 87 57. e-mail:
eirdk@hotmail.com.

Mexico City: EIR, Sor Juana Inés de la Cruz 242-2
Col. Agricultura C.P. 11360
Delegación M. Hidalgo, México D.F.
Tel. (5525) 5318-2301
eirmexico@gmail.com

Canada Post Publication Sales Agreement
#40683579

Postmaster: Send all address changes to *EIR*, P.O.
Box 17390, Washington, D.C. 20041-0390.

Signed articles in *EIR* represent the views of the
authors, and not necessarily those of the Editorial
Board.

The Manhattan Project

Hillary Must Expose Obama's Benghazi Lies

Special to EIR

July 29—Former Secretary of State Hillary Clinton has it in her power to stop President Barack Obama from launching a strategic conflict with Russia, that will, in all likelihood, lead to a thermonuclear war of extinction. All she has to do is come forward with the full truth about Benghazi, starting with the events of September 11, 2012.

Lyndon LaRouche has warned, repeatedly, in recent weeks, that President Obama is prepared to launch a provocation against Russia that would rapidly lead to a general war. The most likely time-frame for such a provocation is the month of August, when the U.S. Congress is in recess, and when the Joint Chiefs of Staff is going through a top-down personnel change. The only thing that can stop this plunge into a thermonuclear war is the removal of President Obama from office, or, in the alternative, a thorough discrediting of the President, to the degree that he is unable to launch the intended provocation, and his resignation or impeachment is imminent.

That is the stark reality of the coming days and weeks. And former Secretary of State Clinton, now a candidate for the Democratic Party presidential nomination, is in a unique position to stop the drive for war by, at long last, telling the truth about Benghazi.

The Benghazi Lies and What Hillary Clinton Knows

On the afternoon of Sept. 11, 2012, well-armed terrorists, affiliated with al-Qaeda, launched a pre-planned assault on the U.S. diplomatic compound in Benghazi, Libya. After an extended fire-fight with the handful of American security personnel guarding U.S. Ambassador Christopher Stevens, the compound was set on fire, and Ambassador Stevens and one other American diplomat were killed. A second U.S. facility in Benghazi, a

CIA compound a mile away from the U.S. mission, was subsequently attacked, resulting in the deaths of two more American officials.

From the instant the attack was launched, Americans on the ground in Benghazi and at the U.S. embassy in Tripoli, Libya, knew that the attack was an armed terrorist assault. Cables between Tripoli and Washington, directed to the National Security Council, the State Department Operations Center, the Pentagon, the CIA, and the Office of the Director of National Intelligence, identified the al-Qaeda-affiliated Ansar al-Sharia cell in the Derna-Benghazi area as the attackers.

In testimony before the U.S. Congress, Gregory Hicks, the deputy chief of mission at the U.S. Embassy in Tripoli, said that he provided a stream of live reports on the ongoing attack every fifteen minutes to the State Department Operations Center, throughout the evening of 9/11/12.

At no time was there any report of a "spontaneous demonstration" outside the Benghazi diplomatic compound. From the very outset, it was clear that the compound was under attack from al-Qaeda.

It was the eleventh anniversary of the original 9/11 attacks. U.S. Presidential elections were weeks away. American drone strikes in the Afghanistan-Pakistan border region had, in June 2012, killed a top al-Qaeda terrorist from Libya; and al-Qaeda leader Ayman al-Zawahiri had issued an order for revenge attacks against the United States for the al-Libi killing on the anniversary of 9/11.

There had been clear advance warnings of trouble in Benghazi and threats to American diplomats for months, even preceding the al-Qaeda threats. The International Committee of the Red Cross had pulled out of Benghazi months before the attack, due to security threats and actual attacks. The British Ambassador and the entire British mission had been shut down in Benghazi, after a bazooka attack on the ambassador's convoy months earlier.

All of this information had been circulated throughout the U.S. Government, through a series of State Department security assessments, which had been regularly updated prior to the 9/11/12 attacks in Benghazi. Over 100 pages of those State Department cables and memos were released to the public within weeks of the Benghazi attack, providing clear evidence of the security crisis in eastern Libya prior to 9/11/12.

Author Edward Klein assembled detailed, eyewitness accounts of the events in Benghazi, Tripoli, and Washington on Sept. 11, 2012. Those details were presented in a chapter in his June 2014 book *Blood Feud*. *Executive Intelligence Review* independently corroborated many of the key details in the Klein account, both before and after its publication, drawing upon U.S. government sources and documents.

In fact, on the morning after the 9/11/12 attacks in Benghazi, *EIR* had received a detailed account of the pre-meditated attack the day before, from a senior U.S. intelligence source, who had been up all night receiving reports from diplomatic sources from the region.

The Essential Facts

The essential facts are as follows:

At 6 p.m. on Sept. 11, 2012, Secretary of State Clinton and a team of top State Department aides received a detailed briefing from DCM Hicks, providing an up-to-the-minute account of the heavily-armed, well-planned assault on the mission. There was no mention of any prior protests, just a detailed report on the terrorist attack, and initial reports that Ansar al-Sharia had made claims over the Internet, that they were responsible for the assault. A short cable from Tripoli to Washington, circulated to all relevant U.S. national security, diplomatic and military agencies, cited the Ansar al-Sharia role.

According to top aides to Secretary Clinton, at 10 p.m. on Sept. 11, 2012, President Obama placed a personal call to Secretary Clinton, ordering her to issue a press release, claiming that the attack on the U.S. compound had been a "spontaneous protest" directed against the recent release of a video slandering the Prophet Mohammed.

In a June 22, 2014 article in the New York Post,

summarizing his investigative findings, Edward Klein wrote:

By 10 p.m. on Sept. 11, 2012, when Hillary Clinton received a call from President Obama, she was one of the most thoroughly briefed officials in Washington on the unfolding disaster in Benghazi, Libya. She knew that Ambassador Christopher Stevens and a communications operator were dead, and that the attackers had launched a well-coordinated mortar assault on the CIA annex, which would cost the lives of two more Americans.

She had no doubt that a terrorist attack had been launched against America on the anniversary of 9/11. However, when Hillary picked up the phone and heard Obama's voice, she learned the president had other ideas in mind. With less than two months before Election Day, he was still boasting that he had al Qaeda on the run.

Klein interviewed one of Secretary Clinton's top legal advisers, who told him:

Obama wanted her to say that the attack had been a spontaneous demonstration triggered by an obscure video on the Internet that demeaned the Prophet Mohammed. Hillary told Obama, "Mr. President, that story isn't credible. Among other things, it ignores the fact that the attack occurred on 9/11." But the President was adamant. He said, "Hillary, I need you to put out a State Department release as soon as possible."

Secretary Clinton promised to call back the President after considering her options. According to the Klein account, based on his interviews with Clinton aides who were present as the events unfolded, Clinton called her husband, who confirmed Hillary's assessment that the Presidential bogus account was not credible. Ex-President Bill Clinton was quoted by Klein's sources, saying: "It's an impossible story. I can't believe the president is claiming it wasn't terrorism. Then again, maybe I can. It looks like Obama isn't going to allow anyone to say that terrorism has occurred on his watch."

Ultimately, Secretary Clinton made a rotten compromise. Realizing that if she did the right thing—

which would have been to publicly resign, in protest over the President's order to lie about the most devastating terrorist attack on the United States since the original 9/11 attacks—Obama would lose re-election, she would be blamed, and her own prospects for winning the presidency would be down the drain, she capitulated.

Shortly after 10 p.m. on the night of Sept. 11, 2012, Hillary Clinton issued the first public statement from the Obama Administration, claiming the attack was "spontaneous" and motivated by the video slander.

Mankind Facing Extinction

Nothing can be done to un-do what Hillary Clinton did, under Obama orders, on the night of 9/11/12. Hillary Clinton has been subpoenaed to appear before the House Select Committee on Benghazi in October to testify under oath. Sometime prior to her appearance, Cheryl Mills, who was her Chief of Staff at the time of the 9/11/12 attacks, and had earlier served as White House General Counsel under President Bill Clinton, will testify under oath.

There is no question that, ultimately, the full truth about Obama's despicable behavior on Benghazi will come out. The crucial question is: When will the truth be revealed and Obama brought down?

If the day of reckoning is postponed until the Congressional inquest takes the Mills and Clinton testimony in October, there may be no Congress. There may be no United States. Mankind may have already been extinguished in a thermonuclear war that will be over in a matter of days, with much of humanity wiped out in the course of that exchange of thermonuclear strikes.

In a very real sense, the fate of mankind is on the line. The only option is for Hillary Clinton to step forward now. She is the crucial eyewitness to the President's willful lies. She can deliver irrefutable testimony, buttressed by other top State Department officials.

It will mean the end of Hillary Clinton's campaign for President, but it will also mean the end of the Obama presidency—before he is able to launch the provocations that could wipe out mankind.

For Hillary Clinton, there is only one right thing to do, and time is fast running out.

EIR Contents

www.larouchepub.com Volume 42, Number 30, July 31, 2015

Cover This Week

'Mountains of Manhattan' by Colin Campbell Cooper (1856-1937)

The Morality of Placement In the Singing Voice

by Lyndon H. LaRouche, Jr.

The following are excerpted, edited remarks made by Lyndon LaRouche on July 25, in reference to the now-unfolding process of building a great Classical choral movement centered in Manhattan.

The Manhattan challenge is what I've been working on, as I said, and one of the things that we're featuring that we're working on, is the question of music. My view is, that if you had people who were being in the process of qualifying as trained in Classical musicianship, and you had a total number of people—oh, about more than 1,500 people—and if you put them to work, you would find that a great number of them would not be qualified as actually singers. But they would have an affinity to the idea of Classical music; and they would think about these things, and they would actually be impassioned about this sort of thing, even though they were not able to sustain a singing voice of competence.

So if you could have about 1,500 people in the New York area, and you could probably have, out of that, you could have something less than 100 who are actually qualified for singing performances. And you put them in the right area of Manhattan in general, so it's convenient for them to convene to experiment and select themselves. You would have the people who did not have well-placed voices, but wanted to be in it; and they would be part of the audience, and they would also try to be training. Because maybe you can get them over the edge there in the quality of the singing voice.

But with that kind of principle, under the condition that you place the voice properly, you don't want to just make noises; you don't want to make frogs in the wintertime. And therefore, you want voices that can be developed and be sustained and can handle the subject matter; because some of the work is very difficult.

But the placing of the voice is what the crucial thing is. If you don't have the proper placing of the voice, it does not work.

Now, there are various degrees of the ability of placing the voice. But once people are in that direction, they can improve to come up to the proper kind of

EIRNS
Panel from the choir loft in the Florence Cathedral, sculpted in marble by Luca della Robbia, 1431-38.

training. Now, I think that what I'm shooting at is, if you have those kinds of choral voices—we've been trying to do it in Manhattan now, same area, midtown—we can actually develop something. In the process of developing it, we can actually define a new way from what we're doing now: a new way to understand what the meaning of music is. Because, what we dealt with, will work; it can work, the principle is there.

And that development of the singing voice, and the ability to take on repertoires which are more and more challenging: that creates something.

Inspiring a Change

Now, what is created? It's not a matter of making noises; it's a matter of the placement as such, the placement of the singing voice. And that is as Furtwängler did in his example [postwar performances of Schubert's Symphony No. 9]. The thing is convenient; the recording of Furtwängler's treatment, is something that is adequate to do that kind of job. What you want to do is, you want to get people out of the idea of being practical, because practical people are inherently stupid people. That is, they don't have anything in themselves which defines them as in the process of meaningful expressions.

And therefore,... we want that kind of thing, where the placement of the singing voice—real placement, not making noises, not throwing their throat out all over the place, but actually placing the voice. When people place the voice well in the process of choral singing, you get an effect which is otherwise inaccessible. And therefore, if we have, say, that number of voices, then we can do it.

And when people learn how to use the singing voice properly, not as throat-throwing things, but the actual placement of the voice, you have a change in the attitude of the people, where they are inspired. Because they're not trying to think about the noises they're making; they're going through the experience of placing the voice. And when they start to place the voice, their attitude about life changes. And therefore, the purpose is to use that factor, the placement of the voice, the placement of the singing voice in a competent placement, to effect changes in the mental outlook of the population. It affects the people who can do the choral work, the soloists' work, the choral work in general; and those who can partici-pate in hearing the experience of the choral production.

In other words, if you don't want to sing the note—what you call the note—you don't want to bellow out the note. That is not a good idea! But if you could place the idea in the mind in such a way that the voice is now in accord with that placement, you change the attitude on life of the people.

First of all, you've changed the choral group of the singers; and then you affect those who are not such good singers. And they will tend to hear what they cannot project; or not project efficiently.

And that attitude is the basis for morality.

Some Further Remarks On Placement in Classical Singing

by John Sigerson

July 26—It would be obvious to the informed reader of Lyndon LaRouche's remarks above, that the concept of "placement" that LaRouche is presenting extends far beyond the typical music instructor's usual understanding of that term.

For the benefit of those who may not be familiar with even the restricted use of the concept: Placement is one of the many fruits of the Italian Renaissance of the Fifteenth Century which rescued western civilization from the chaos and mass death of the preceding century, and which saw the birth of modern science through the work of Nicholas of Cusa (1401-1464), supported by composers of polyphonic vocal music such as Guillaume Dufay (1397-1474), and later successors such as Josquin des Prez (1450-1521). New potentials of the human singing voice were discovered and developed, as most prominently celebrated in the meticulous sculptures by Luca della Robbia (1399-1482) on the choir stall of the Santa Maria del Fiore cathedral in Florence, showing a choir of singers with such accuracy that one can, when viewing those figures, identify the species of each singer's voice—bass, tenor, alto, soprano—and even the particular vowel which each is singing.

As Leonardo da Vinci (1452-1519) documented in one of his notebook sketches, the singing of each vowel was associated with a specific "placement," which is not a physical location *per se*, but rather is a mental image of a particular location in the singer's head, which the singer imagines in order to "place" each voiced syllable in such a way that not only can it be sustained with maximum beauty, but also towards which the singer can easily move from a preceding intoned vowel, and then move with equal ease to the succeeding one.

Therefore, even in this restricted sense, proper placement is never just a matter of "where" to sing individual notes, but rather it is a mental aid for moving the voice as one proceeds through a musical-poetic phrase.

The concept is not restricted to singers. Great speakers (think of Franklin D. Roosevelt, or Martin Luther King) would employ the same concept of placement—something which, if you haven't noticed, is completely lacking in recent Presidents and public figures! Even players of musical instruments employ this concept—especially those who have not forgotten that musical instruments are not just mechanical things, but must always be coerced into imitating and extending the best qualities of the human singing voice. An instrumentalist who cannot, or will not make their instrument "sing," is a failed artist.

Over the centuries since the Italian Renaissance, many singers and singing teachers have promoted their own particular schemas for exactly "where" the voice must be placed, depending on (a) the vowel (or voiced consonant) being sung, (b) the species of the singer's voice, and (c) the vocal register required to sing the note (and its passage). These schemas are often useful as a starting-point for the beginner; however, as the singer gains more familiarity with the peculiarities of his or her own voice, the thoughtful singer will develop his or her own personal mental map of placement. Singers, on the other hand, who insist on continuing to cling to a fixed mental schema, are never able to develop the freedom of placement which is absolutely required in order to convey a true musical idea to an audience.

I should also add at this point, that as the result of Johannes Kepler's discovery of the principles of the Solar System—principles which include the same con-

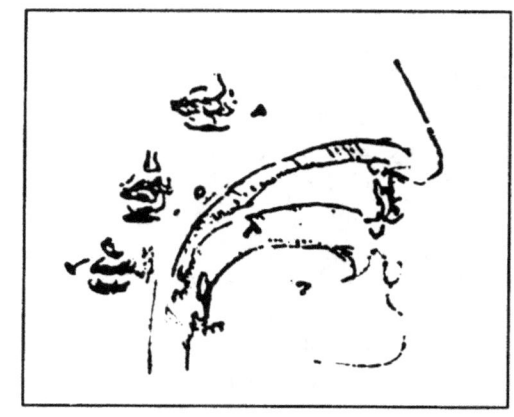

a	e	i	o	u
ba	be	bi	bo	bu
ca	ce	ci	co	cu
da	de	di	do	du
e				
fa	fe	fi	fo	fu
ga	ge	gi	go	gu
la	le	li	lo	lu
ma	me	mi	mo	mu
na	ne	ni	no	nu
pa	pe	pi	po	pu
qa	qe	qi	qo	qu
ra	re	ri	ro	ru
sa	se	si	so	su
ta	te	ti	to	tu

Schiller Institute

The drawing and listing here comes from Leonardo da Vinci's "Anatomy Manuscripts," in which he studied how human language reflects the natural beauty of the universe. The drawing shows Leonardo's concept of where in the mouth the various vowels are produced.

cept of placement and registration as described above!—it became irrefutable to the best singers and composers that vocal placement requires that the values of the musical scale be tuned such that "middle C" is located very close to 256 cycles per second. This "natural" or "scientific" tuning, which later came to be known as the "Verdi tuning" because Giuseppe Verdi insisted upon it, uniquely locates the main register-shifts around the points of maximum "stress" in the well-tempered musical domain.

All the great Classical composers from Johann Sebastian Bach onward used this scientific "natural" tuning as their mental reference-point for composing for the voice, even at times when the instruments available to them may have been tuned differently. For an in-depth examination of these principles of

Famed Italian baritone Piero Cappuccilli demonstrates Classical tuning during an April 1988 conference on tuning sponsored by the Schiller Institute.

tuning and registration, see the book which I co-authored, *A Manual on the Rudiments of Tuning and Registration.*[1]

True Placement

Therefore, even in its more restricted sense, only human beings consciously employ placement. Animals—and human beings who insist on acting like animals—simply push out sounds as an immediate expression of their wants and needs, with no *forethought* given to *how* the vocalization is to be shaped.

LaRouche's concept, moreover, goes far beyond this, because he identifies placement as unique to human *creative* mentation, and to the communication of principles which increase the human species' mastery of our Solar System, and of our Galaxy, and beyond!

This kind of placement is therefore something very special. It is the true gate, as it were, into the realm of the empyreal, or what some may identify as "deeply religious." Even though the great works of Classical polyphony of Bach, Haydn, Beethoven, Schubert, Schumann, and Brahms cry out for it, it is

---

1. *A Manual on the Rudiments of Tuning and Registration* is available for purchase, along with extra features, on DVD, at the LaRouche Publications store, store.larouchepub.com.

but rarely encountered in musical performances today,—though many have attempted to "fake it." That is not only the fault of the performers, but also of modern "dumbed-down" and jaded audiences, who want to hear "new, more exciting sounds," but are deaf to the placement of true m u s i c — p l a c e m e n t which, in fact, is entirely in the mind, and, thus, soundless.

Precisely because this placement is beyond the ken of most people today, LaRouche's recommendation has always been to focus on a handful of the very best examples of it in audio recordings of past times, when it was still being employed by the few "hold-outs" still committed to keeping alive true Classical composition, which had all but expired with the death of Johannes Brahms in 1897.

Most notable among these are the post-World War II recordings of Schubert's Symphony No. 9 as performed by Wilhelm Furtwängler (1886-1954). Another is the 1950 recording of *Vier ernste Gesänge* (*Four Serious Songs*) by Brahms, performed under Furtwängler's tutelage by the young baritone Dietrich Fischer-Dieskau. Yet another is Furtwängler's 1938 recording of Pyotr Tchaikovsky's Symphony No. 6, a recording which played an important role in LaRouche's own thinking, because it demonstrates how even a lesser composer such as Tchaikovsky (whom Furtwängler once described as a *ein halb-Symphoniker*—"a halfway symphonist") could be brought to Classical levels of placement under a placement-master's hand.

And to complete this handful of recordings, there are those of the best singers of Classical German *Lieder* (songs), most notably Heinrich Schlusnus (1888-1952).

Like in a bright light, it may take your mental eyes some time to adjust to hearing not just the sounds of these recordings, but rather the soundless ideas behind, or between the sounds. Here is not the place to offer a

EIRNS

The author leads a men's chorus, singing the Prisoners' chorus from Beethoven's Fidelio, in New Jersey on July 24, 2015.

detailed discussion of these recordings; that is best left to study groups, listening and discussing together—far better than private listening on a computer or portable device.

But, a hint on Schubert's Symphony No. 9: Terribly banal modern performances of this work are frequently heard on so-called Classical radio stations. However, your first experience of Furtwängler's performance of this huge symphony might be overwhelming. Take your time! In the second movement, for example, familiarize yourself with its various phases, and then listen carefully to how Furtwängler moves from one phase to the next. That's where you will experience true placement in action.

Those in the greater New York area have an additional opportunity to study Schubert's great symphony: They can attend the Saturday "Manhattan Project" dialogues with Lyndon LaRouche, which always begin with a choral voyage of discovery led by its choral director Diane Sare.

The Manhattan Project's Choral Voice

In today's collapsing culture, merely coming together to sing choral works, even those by great Classical composers, is not enough to achieve true placement. That is because the singers generally have come together for private reasons, and are never really challenged to rise above their private concerns (or obses-

sions), and to create a *unity of purpose* which can be none other than raising the moral quality of human culture in general. In that sense, achieving placement is therefore an intensely "political" challenge!

To put a fine point on it: A chorus consisting primarily of singers who believe that a President Obama is "not all that bad," will *never* be able to achieve true placement! And likewise with a chorus of people who "like Classical music," but who then go home and "relax" to the most degenerate kinds of popular filth.

This is not some sort of "moral code" to be adhered to "for the sake of the cause," but rather is an inescapable feature of the perilous condition of humanity today. Dropping one's addiction to popular culture may seem difficult, but as with any addiction, beating it will be the only certain way to reverse the otherwise inevitable collapse of our culture, and the probable extinction of human civilization in a thermonuclear holocaust.

Hand-in-hand with this unity of purpose goes the vocal unity of each choral section—bass, tenor, alto, soprano—and sub-section. The individual singer must be willing to surrender his or her own self-imposed limitations—"I can only sing that passage when I sing it loud!"—"How dare you ask me to sing with more/less vibrato on that passage!"—to the requirements of the placement of the choral voice. In some cases, this may even require the singer to completely re-examine and revise his or her firmly held concept of "This is the only way I can place my voice." Singers need to be able to laugh as they overcome their own limitations; and there must be free and open discussions of these matters, with no backbiting or gossip permitted.

Such is the climate that can foster the attitude which, as LaRouche states, "is the basis for morality" of chorus and audience alike.

LaRouche in Dialogue With the Manhattan Project On the Threatened Edge of A Thermonuclear War

Saturday, July 25, 2015. Below are edited excerpts of Lyndon LaRouche's dialogue with the Manhattan Project.

Dennis Speed:: My name is Dennis Speed, and on behalf of the LaRouche Political Action Committee, I want to welcome you to our ongoing Manhattan Project Dialogue with Lyndon LaRouche. The recent NASA New Horizons mission to Plato—excuse me!—Pluto has once again reminded us of what LaRouche often says, which is that it is impossible to understand what's going on on our planet, or in our Solar System, unless you have an understanding, or at least begin to try to discover, how our Galaxy works. And that includes understanding anything about political life.

What we're going to do is we're going to get a statement, an opening statement, from Lyn, and then it will be followed immediately by our questions. And I know some people are here for the first time, so what we are going to do is to invite you to ask questions, and we'll go right to that after our opening statement. So, Lyn?

Lyndon LaRouche: Well, good afternoon. I'm still alive, which, I suppose, at my age is always news, as opposed to other options.

We're in a very serious situation. We're on the threatened edge of a thermonuclear war. We don't know exactly when that thermonuclear war will break out, but we do have a sense that it's fairly soon, unless certain developments occur, including those which are very important in terms of the United States itself, which now faces the question of what is going to be the termi-

nation of the current President of the United States, who must be withdrawn from his office, if we are to escape his role, and that of the British Empire, as a threat for global thermonuclear warfare.

And thermonuclear warfare today, in today's circumstances, means that the war is launched, in this case, from probably President Obama. And the war would be unfolded very rapidly from that point on. At that point, in the present plan of things, Russia would be ready to react the minute that a U.S. thermonuclear war attack had been launched. It would be in less than minutes. And at that point, therefore, there would be very few living persons on this planet.

Real Extinction War

So, the mission now is to take the steps, especially inside the United States itself, to bring Obama out of power, and to bring in forces which are now trying to build themselves, and express themselves, in the course of the oncoming election process. And we hope that our role in the United States, in conjunction with other parts of the planet, will ensure that that thermonuclear war, which would be a real extinction war, should not happen.

Therefore that means that political measures have to be taken, especially inside the United States, *especially* inside the United States, to ensure that Obama, or Obama's policy of his incumbency, not continue to be the ruling force inside the United States. Because *that*— what Obama represents—is, above all else, the immediate source of a threatened thermonuclear war, or

"What Obama represents is, above all else, the immediate source of a threatened thermonuclear war," said LaRouche. Here, Obama announces the nomination of Gen. Joseph Dunford for Chairman of the Joint Chiefs of Staff. In his Senate hearing, Dunford directly accused Russia of being "the greatest threat" to the United States.

whatever might be his successor.

So that's the real issue. We now have to consider the considerations which *we*, in the United States, and elsewhere, must take into account to prevent what has been heretofore the British Monarchy's, and Obama's, intention toward a general war, launched against Russia, from the United States. And so everything really centers on that issue. So, let's discuss such matters.

Speed: Okay, very good. We have our first question.

Q: Hello, Lyndon. I am Kay S—. I do have a question, but first I want to make a statement about what I believe. It is my opinion that we never won the Revolutionary War. It's true that we won the military part, and it's true that the British recognized that they could not beat us militarily, but they did set up a subtle political strategy such that they have taken control over this country in many different ways, very quietly. And they are still here. If, not "if" but when—the House of Windsor falls, and you say that Obama will go down too, there's still going to be a lot of their strategy remaining in the country, and how do you see it, the country being evolved into what we were meant to be?

LaRouche: Well, I have a very definite conception of what this is, and it comes from—you know, I'm sort of an antiquated creature right now, but I have a lot of experience as a result of being an antiquated creature, and I'm still alive and active, and I have a lot of knowledge about these matters. Which is one of the benefits of the side of old age, in my case.

British Monarchy Collapsing

We do have the option, if we can move the political processes within the United States, on the one side, in the right way, and if we can induce the British Empire as such, to disintegrate itself. Now these possibilities are realistic, and rather immediate. The British Monarchy, the British Empire thus, therefore, is in the process of collapsing, of disintegrating, and that would be a very, very good thing.

Unfortunately, most of Europe is under the influence of what has been the British Empire. There is practically no nation in Southern and Western Europe which is not polluted with the effects of the British Empire's influence over the European nations in particular. This is not quite the same thing with Russia. Russia has a somewhat better situation, because of its connection with China, and with India, and with other countries. And also some nations in South America, and a couple of nations in the southern part of the Mediterranean.

These things are possible, they're good possibilities, but we must actually create both a new government *in* the United States, to get rid of the Obama Administration, and the Bush tradition as such. We must quickly organize around Glass-Steagall, as a crucial issue. In other words, Glass-Steagall is important not just as some kind of gimmick, but it's important because of what it has done, how Glass-Steagall was established by President Franklin Roosevelt. Without Franklin Roosevelt's forecasting, we probably would not have made it as a nation this far.

So, the important thing is, we must have—if we want to be practical—we must have an approach by the forces in the United States, which are not those of the Bush family, and not those of Obama, and not those of any of the supporters of Bush or Obama, or allies of Bush and Obama. That's the precondition. If we do that, inside the United States—because the British Monarchy is now in the process of disintegrating, and that is a very good thing—to get rid of the British Monarchy.

Because the British Monarchy is actually a Nazi operation, or became known as a Nazi operation during the course of the Twentieth Century. That's very clearly so. It launched World War I and World War II, and also went on before World War I, in that decade. So the time has come that we in the United States, with those with whom we can share a common intention for the benefit of mankind, for the economic development of the conditions of life of the human being, [can achieve] the progress of humanity to meet the new challenges which are to be met in what's confronting us now, with what's recently happened in the northern part of our territory, and in terms of the Galaxy.

Manhattan the Last Bastion

We're now at a point where we must organize ourselves, throughout a new system of global governmental action and correction. We must have that, and I think we can do that. I think it's possible. I think the right ideas are shaping into performance now, the possibility. And I've spent most of my life on this subject, and I'm kind of an old geezer right now, but I'm still lively, and I'm still doing things, and I will do things. But I think we have to have a perspective among our citizens, in particular, and among appropriate selected leaders of our system of government inside the United States, in particular. That is what is required.

We're on the very edge of a threatened extinction, or virtual extinction, of the human species. And we have to be serious about this. And we have to build up, as I would emphasize, in the area of Manhattan. Because Manhattan is the last surviving area with any kind of authority in terms of our tradition—say, the tradition of Alexander Hamilton. And today, despite all the corruption which exists in Manhattan, among the institutions there, the fact of the matter—this is a last bastion of defense of what the United States has represented since Alexander Hamilton did his job.

Q: The thing that needs to be taken care of is the education. The education brainwashed the children that were in the schools. I could see it in one of my sons in particular. He went to a prestigious high school, and came out completely brainwashed. Academically, it

Martin O'Malley's facebook page

Instituting Glass-Steagall is the only thing which can give stability to the United States. Here, candidate for the Democratic Party nomination for President Martin O'Malley, who is consistently campaigning for Glass-Steagall's reinstatement.

was a wonderful education. It seems to me that would be one of the first places that has to be changed, among, I'm sure, many others as well.

Reinstitute Glass-Steagall

LaRouche: I think I would say that Manhattan, despite the problems in Manhattan—I'm quite aware of them; I once lived for some time in Manhattan and had more or less important positions during that process—so I would say, yes. That Manhattan as such contains within it, a tradition of the type which is needed right now.

There are some people, members of the Congress, and especially the Senate, and some candidates for Presidential or related nomination, who are valuable. But we need to get rid of the Bush-Obama legacy in the United States; because that's the particular disease—the Bush-Obama legacy. If we do that, we get rid of some of that stuff, and institute Glass-Steagall as a law immediately, then Glass-Steagall is the only thing now which can create stability for the United States.

You have to know that in Britain, for example, in most of Europe, and throughout the United States, Glass-Steagall is indispensable for recreating the economy. And the economy is not just an abstract thing; the economy is a process of progressive development of the economic powers of the citizen, their intellectual development, and their powers of new skills at a higher level appropriate to dealing with the great crises which are occurring throughout the planet. Because we do have crises throughout the planet right now; most of it at least. We have some good developments in South America—parts of South America. We have good developments in China; excellent developments in China. We have a new renaissance of India; we have a renaissance in Russia. And we have the possibility of surviving a re-borning of some of the nations of Europe; and so forth and so on.

So, we have the options; but we need the leadership. And my problem has always been to get the economy organized on the basis of a principle which I know very well; which I used to know from experience. But I haven't been too familiar with that stuff since the Bush family came into power, during the course of that period of life.

Q: [followup] I grew up under Glass-Steagall and I truly appreciate its value. Thank you.

LaRouche: Certainly.

Q: Hi Lyn, it's A— from New York. On the Thursday call [Fireside Chat], your latest statement on "Waking Up the Sleepwalkers" was read, and I've read it a couple of times since. And I'm forwarding it and trying to now have all my contacts read this, because I believe it to be a mirror; very reflective of, first of all, how I used to think and approach things. I laughed a lot throughout, because it was reflective. But I really think that does capture what many otherwise good people and honest people find themselves in; and the type of habits that need to broken in the thinking of the individual.

I'm not going to read the paper, but people have too many facts and fraudulent information that clutters up their attention. So, the reality of the impending threat of something like thermonuclear war,—there's so much clutter there, that besides fear, it's hard for them to actually see this. And now, with the Brits on the way out; this is something none of us have ever experienced before. How do I now turn to those contacts that I wish to become more active, and show them this is indeed what you're forecasting; and how do we move to bring about that happy occasion?

The Crisis of 1890

LaRouche: Well, first of all, you have to take into account a few facts; facts which are unfortunately rather rarely known. Now, what's happened is this: There was a great crisis toward the end of the Nineteenth Century; that is, before the Twentieth Century and now the

Twenty-first Century. But in that period, which was a decade after Bismarck was junked by the influence of the British Empire, and when Bismarck was thrown out of office, we had the birth of a series of assassinations. Like the assassination of the President of France at the beginning of the 1890s.

So, at that point, we came into a period of orchestrated war; because Bismarck was no longer in power. And the fact that Bismarck was kicked out of power under the orders of the British monarchy, and by a new chief of the government of a British-supplied ruler of Germany, meant war; and a general war began. It began in France against the President of France. It began in other places; wars, medium-scale wars, larger wars increasing going into the beginning of the Twentieth Century. And since the Twentieth Century, of course, you had the preconditions of World War I, so-called; and from there, we went to World War II. And in this process, the planet went through a moral degeneration, which came in the late 1890s. And this thing caused a shift in policy in the modern civilization which went against sanity as such. Warfare, yes.

We had a revival of the idea of economy under President Franklin Roosevelt, with his less than four full terms of office. He was a founder who saved us during that interval of the early part of the Twentieth Century. Now in that process, what was introduced was called economy; and economy was simply a racket. And therefore, what you had is, you had a continuing decline in the productive powers of labor; that is, the mental productive powers of labor have been running down at a generally accelerating rate over the course since Roosevelt's Presidency. But then over the course of the Twentieth Century, and now the real collapse in this present century.

The True Basis for Economy

What has happened is, the demoralization of the economy; the degeneration of the intellectual life of the citizens of the United States in particular. Because you have on the one hand, the Wall Street crowd; who are actually a pack of thieves. They always were a pack of thieves; and they often turn out to be Republicans, which is not a very good thing to happen to us as a nation.

So, the problem we have, is that there's still support for a financial system of the type which now exists in the United States. We have to eliminate the policies of economy which have predominated over the course of the Twentieth Century, and now into the Twenty-First

Century. What that means is, instead of relying on the system of money—money as such; money as such is not a legitimate basis for economy. The basis lies in the collective powers and creative powers of the citizens of the world; the citizens of our own nation in particular.

We are now destroying the minds of our people. We are destroying our youth systematically in the recent succession of terms of birth. We're declining; every generation is poorer and more stupid and more corrupt than the previous one. So, this is what we're up against. We need a transformation in the policy of our government and other governments; the nations of the planet, the leading nations of the planet. We have to go back away from the idea of the practical idea, with business as usual. And we have to go back to a science driver program; that is, the idea that every person should be increasing their productive powers of labor, mentally, throughout the course of life up to the point of the end of their lifespan. But each generation must be superior in its level of productive achievement, one after the other. And that's the only solution.

Eliminate Wall Street

So therefore, if you don't get rid of Wall Street, and you don't restore Glass-Steagall as a protection against Wall Street; then the fate of the United States is a horrible one. And we're on the edge now, that we must recognize that the destructive force of Wall Street—which should never have existed—must be eliminated. And we must go back to a principle of physical productivity, not financial productivity. Productive, actually physical productive things; the increase of the powers of labor, the increase of the mental powers of labor, the fruits of such labor. These are the instruments which must be restored to action if there's going to be any moral encouragement for survival of the United States in particular, but also for many other nations and the world as a whole. That's the situation.

Q: Good afternoon, Lyn. I did want to let people here in the meeting and also in the audience know that as the result of what we've done over the past few years around Glass-Steagall, particularly getting the introduction of New Jersey Senate and Assembly resolutions put forward, one of the co-signers to that legislation on becoming a member of the Congress, has just within the past few days, signed on to the Glass-Steagall legislation in Washington. In fact, I've been in the last few days meeting with a number of the Assembly and Senate representatives there still.

Clearly, what had occurred during that beginning of the Roosevelt Administration, was clearly a joyful period in American history. That people were getting relief. And it's also of note that it was in Philadelphia, where when JP Morgan and others had attempted the coup against the Roosevelt Administration, the newspapers in that area published the behind-the-scenes goings-on of JP Morgan and others that had attempted to bring down the Roosevelt Administration.

I think we see the same kind of thing now going on with the exposure of the Royal Family and all of the tentacles that they had put out throughout Europe and elsewhere, including here in the United States with the Bush family, that seems to be of extreme significance now, that they are directly both looking at that Roosevelt means of going after and creating a new world climate. That's the situation right now. And I'd just like your thoughts on that.

Mathematics is Crap

LaRouche: OK, the point is, we have to look at the focal point, of the idea of money as such, which is really a curse, because, when we measure this in monetary terms, you are acting like an animal, not a human being. The animal has no ability to create creativity in the sense that the human species has a natural ability to advance the productive powers of labor. By the productive powers of labor you mean the ability of one generation to be smarter in practice than the previous generation, which means new technologies—not just technologies, but new discoveries of universal physical principle.

And we're talking about something which happened back during the Renaissance period, where Nicolaus of Cusa was a leading figure among others, and those who followed him, and the great Renaissance that occurred in that time. Now that was *crushed* in the succeeding century, in the beginning of the new century. It was done deliberately. And even Christianity as a belief was morally destroyed during that century. Then Kepler came along, and Kepler discovered the Solar System. He proved the principle of the existence of a Solar System. Then he had a follower, Leibniz. And Leibniz was the man of a century, a literal century, who created the greatest rates of progress of mankind, in that part of the world, at that time and later.

What is important is the increase of the productive powers of mankind, that is, the creative powers. For example, scientific creativity, new principles. All right, we went to Kepler; Kepler was the person who defined

creative commons

Money vs. Production: *As long as money power, such as that wielded by J.P. Morgan-Chase, the biggest derivatives bank in the U.S. (shown here at 23 Wall Street), dominates the world, it will sabotage the development of the productive powers of labor (as expressed by this welder).*

the meaning of Solar System. Now we have the Galactic System. The Galactic System—our supply of water on Earth depends not on Earth as such. Yes, the water on Earth is very important to us. *But!* The real source of the power to increase the power of mankind in the Solar System and beyond lies, in that kind of technology and that kind of progress—Galactic principles, following that.

So therefore, we don't do things like mathematics. Mathematics is crap, inherently, because it's stagnant; it's inherently stagnant. The idea that you have practical mathematical methods for progress—that is really a myth. And you see what the result is. The result is in the course of the Twentieth Century since Franklin Roosevelt, the general trend in the conditions of life in the United States is downward. Oh, some nice things happened, but it's downward. The educational system—downward. The young people entering schools are dumber than their predecessors. And that's the policy.

The Science-Driver

So trying to be practical in these matters is stupid. It is the development of principles of physical science and what that means—discoveries of principle—not practical stuff. The practical people are useless people. There are reasons for that. What you need is the end of practical production. And high-technology progress, new conceptions of the principles of the universe,—these are the things on which the progress of mankind has always depended. And beginning with the end of the Nineteenth Century, in the United States and in Europe,

there has been a rather consistent but irregular decline of the mental powers of the members of society, in general. There are exceptions, but in general. China's coming back; India will come back. Nations of South America will improve things if they don't get interference with that.

But the problem is that the people of the United States have been conditioned to accept successive steps of degeneration in the practical application and discovery of the scientific principles on which the continued existence of mankind as a successful species depends. And that's what the problem is. So we need to have a driver program in terms of science—real science, not mathematical science, but real science, the discovery of principles which no mathematician heretofore was ever capable of discovering.

Q: Mr. LaRouche, I'd like to ask a question in regard to some of the rumors that I've heard from military intelligence sources, about a very legitimate threat they believe to the U.S., in this coming September time period, of a false flag operation, and I want to ask if that would be consistent with your concern toward the escalation of a thermonuclear war or World War III. And if that is the situation, how, for example, the science-driven initiatives you're speaking of, such as fission and fusion power, could be used to spearhead a course away from this war and financial collapse?

LaRouche: We're now occupying the month of July, going toward August. We're having several developments. On the one hand, we're having a decline of everything, in terms of the United States and in terms of most of Western Europe. The conditions in Europe in general and in North Africa are terrible, and getting worse all the time. The situation in the trans-Atlantic region is bad enough, but the Mediterranean region, the Mediterranean war, is an absolute disaster.

Dump Obama

Now Russia is stabilizing itself, successfully and has a very significant military capability, which it is not going to use to launch a war. But the war was likely to come from two sources—the British Empire sources and those of the United States, under the present government, under the Bush Administrations and under the Obama Administration. The Obama Administration now is the greatest source of threat to the existence of the human species on the planet right now, unless that's dumped. That's what they're headed for.

The British Empire, which has been the source of this evil, is now crumbling, in the sense that there is a revolt against the British Royal Family, and the depth of that revolt goes back to a couple of centuries, since the evil fully dominated the degeneration of civilization.

So what is required, therefore, is to get rid of the problem. And the problem largely, in the United States, is Wall Street. And one of the key problems has been, that Wall Street dominates the Senate, and corrupts the House as well. So the direction is degeneration. The basis for this policy of degeneration is using money *per se* as the standard rather than productivity: that is, actual physically efficient productivity, in the powers of mankind's labor, the improvement of mankind's power of labor. So we're operating on the wrong policy, especially in the Twentieth Century, especially since the end of the '90s in the Twentieth Century.

So the question is, what are we going to do about it? Well, the first thing is, you've got to get rid of Wall Street. Now that's a good thing to do right away. I don't care what happens; Wall Street should be shut down and the monetarism should *cease to be the standard* for measure of economic performance.

The Problem with Wall Street

What happens is that the Wall Street effect reduces the standard of productivity and life of the average citi-

DoD photo courtesy of U.S. Navy

The Obama threat: Deployment of destroyers like this, part of the Aegis Ballistic Missile Defense program, is going ahead right up to the border of Russia, threatening Russia and courting nuclear war. The destroyer shown, the USS Hopper, fires a missile during an exercise in the Pacific in 2009.

zen. They get lower and lower wages, lower and lower conditions of health care, and life in general, and intelligence. Look, the educational system of the United States has been degenerating essentially ever since the death of Franklin Roosevelt. There were some good Presidents who did some good things, but Wall Street and certain institutions of Wall Street have prevented that. The corruption and decay, the decadence of the United States since the end of Roosevelt's Administration, is astonishing! It's massive! The educational system is massively corrupted. The older the person, the more intelligent they are. Why? Because they remember something that the next generation never had a chance to know.

And people are getting cheaper and cheaper and cheaper. They're now being killed. The policy of the British Empire was to reduce the human population, as now the policy there is to reduce the population in total, from seven billion people as of now, to one billion people. Genocide. And we have a pope, a new Pope, who's controlled by the British Empire, and they've set forth a policy, imposed upon that Pope, to reduce the population of the planet by that degree. Mass murder.

So therefore, unless we understand that the idea of a monetarist system, and the idea of practical reduction of the level of standard of life of people—as long as that is not removed and reversed—the prospects for mankind are virtually nil, and that has to be changed.

Q: Good afternoon, Mr. LaRouche, how are you today?

LaRouche: I'm fine. I'm old, but I'm fine.

Q: OK. I must say the Royal Family has been hiding in plain sight for a very long time. Because when I was growing up in the Caribbean, which was part of the colonial system, they taught us about their history, and we go back to the Tudors and Stuarts, the War of the Roses, and I think if America was teaching this type of history, and they went into world geography, America would have been equipped to handle the British Empire now. I think the lack of knowledge has created a problem for America now, because education was more into the color of the skin rather than educating everyone.

I was fortunate enough to get a good education in the Caribbean, and sometimes when I told people certain things, they would say, "Oh, you think you're all that." But it wasn't that; it's the fact that we were taught merely to spy on other people. But, I'm telling you, the time has come now for the world to understand that the British Empire has been the type of country that—they come with diplomacy in the front, and they stir up some very deep trouble in the back. Diplomacy in the front. Let the Queen come and greet you, but you know she has her spies looking out to do a lot of stuff to America.

Now I must say one other thing. If a lot of those politicians were a little more educated in the real things they were supposed to know, America would not have been in the position it is in now.

The Death-Knell of Progress

LaRouche: Yeah, it's true; but the point is, go back to the 1890s. The 1890s was the turning point down, in the United States. We had a President [McKinley] who was killed; and we had this clown, who served two terms as a clown, in the course of the Twentieth Century.

The Twentieth Century, on the American books, has been the death knell of progress in the United States up to the present time. Now [Franklin] Roosevelt did some good things, and some other people as Presidents tried to do some good things, but it's amazing, that the best presidents we ever had tend to be assassinated, under British orders.

So the problem is that we have been living in a world of folly, of believing in the dollar, in monetary values, instead of the creative, productive values. Remember, the characterization of the development of the United States, especially in the course of the Nineteenth Century, had been, despite all evils, and there were many evils, up until the point particularly of Franklin Roosevelt, but the problem is that we don't have a monetary system, shall we say, or an economic system, which is

that of the Twentieth Century. The Twentieth Century has been one big farce, for most of Europe, and for the United States. That is, the standard of productivity, per capita, in the population has been in decline. You can see it in terms of scientific development, people who were still skilled in scientific practice.

There's only one man in the Twentieth Century who really understood the principle of science. And he was pushed aside.

Now, We Have a Program

Now some of these people were very practical people—I knew some of them,—and they were very practical but they were also good, but they didn't get the idea of what real human progress is. They were too much operating based on *mathematics*; and the best thing you can do with mathematics, is sort of burn the books, [laughs] and get back to some principled standards which are human physical standards. Not mathematical standards, human standards. The increase of the productive powers of labor as represented by the applications of physical principles of development, which can be applied by the practice of human beings.

And that's where the problem lies. We have to say, "Now, we have a program." China is moving, with great speed, to progress. India, is kind of mobilizing itself, in kind of a selfish way, but it's done well, in order to get the increase in the productive powers of labor in India. We have an improvement in Egypt, a significant improvement in Egypt, under difficulties, and so forth, and things like that. South American nations are trying to mobilize themselves to move in the direction of progress. Most of these nations do not understand the scientific principle; but they understand the effect of the practice of science when it works.

So what we need to do is we need a true *science-driver outlook*. What do I mean? I mean things like Kepler. Kepler discovered the Solar System, defined it. And that was a great thing. Nicolaus of Cusa had earlier made a great contribution to the principles of scientific progress, as he represented them. But then, boom! We had great contributors, who were the founders of our republic; but since that time, there's been a general tendency toward what became the Twentieth Century. And the Twentieth Century has been the death knell of most of civilization.

Q: I was provoked by your discussion last week, and just have a question, because we're obviously faced with an incredibly revolutionary moment. And although

isro.gov.in

"We need a true science-driver outlook," LaRouche stressed. Here we see that outlook in action in India, with the lift-off of the first experimental suborbital flight of India's latest generation Launch Vehicle-LVM3 in December 2014.

people are participating in it, I think it's still a big question in their mind, as to how you actually achieve victory. My question is about these revolutionary moments as such. Because it seems as if time is going, society is going, according to trends, or principles, or ideas, and then all of a sudden, there's a big change; it's almost like of a magical nature. So what, then, is it? What creates that potential, for a system overhaul, and what is the substance then of these revolutionary moments?

What We're Doing Here Today

LaRouche: Well, you are addressing me directly, aren't you? [laughs] The point is, that we have to develop physical revolutionary progress, not so-called scientific progress in the deductive sense. We have to discover new principles, which means we have to go to various parts of space and discover what's going on out there. And we find out that these kinds of changes,

physical changes, not mathematical ones, physical principle changes which are progressive, or which can show themselves to be progressive; and that's what the whole thing is, has to be, about.

We have to change the thing. Look our educational system, a university educational system is largely, increasingly disastrous, because there's so much on mathematics that they have no competence and no interest in science—that is, in physical science, real science. That's what the problem has been.

And what we're doing now, what you're doing right now in assembling in this meeting which is now ongoing, is exactly that, because that's what *I'm* doing *with* you! I'm trying to create an institution and support the creation of an institution, inside Manhattan, itself, and not exclusively inside Manhattan as such, but there, right now; and we want to create an institution, which *thinks*, an institution which actually *thinks*. It doesn't copy things, it's not a Wall Street institution, but is creating solutions which are physical solutions, not mathematical ones, but *physical* ones, for the improvement of the productive powers of labor of mankind. Or, for health care—you know, science for health care, for example, directly applied as medicine, to the scientific requirements of health care. To promoting longevity, of useful people, in particular. Of having more children, who are better educated, better developed.

Not on the basis of mathematics, but on the basis of discoveries of *physical* principles, not mathematical ones as such. Mathematical functions are really tertiary matters; they may be useful, but only in a tertiary way, not a direct way. And that's the way to look at it.

Speed: This is going to have to be, I believe, our last question. We're running up on time.

How Do We Turn This Around?

Q: Mr. LaRouche, thank you. I agree with everything you're saying, and I understand the need for physical productivity. But there's a situation in this country now where the American citizens are just completely fed up with the ineffectual people that are in Washington. So, although in theory it's great to say that we need to be physically productive, people want something to really sink their teeth into, and they really want to know how this thing is going to get implemented, when everyone in Washington is even—for instance, the Republicans: they said if we have a Republican Senate and a Republican House, they'd be able to pass bills that the American people were passionate about. So we voted all the Republicans into the House and Senate, and nothing got passed that we were asking for!

So now we have Glass-Steagall that's been reintroduced, and so, how does it get passed, when the people in Washington, are tied into the banking system in the way it is now, and are profitting from it? The politicians, and the Senators in Washington now are only concerned, with maintaining their power and keeping their positions. And their pockets full—exactly.

How do we turn this thing around? Your solution is great! I agree with it a hundred percent; people need to be more physically productive, that's great! But right now, there's a sense of expediency, and we feel that we need to know how are we going to get these politicians to really understand that our country is in jeopardy?

If we get a President like Hillary Clinton, Martin O'Malley, or God forbid, Bernie Sanders, we might as well put the last nail in America's coffin. Because we are really in dire straits now and there's a sense of *revolution* going on! I'm online all the time! I go on Facebook, I go on different sites, I listen to conservative radio. I'm conservative, I have no use for the liberals—I'm sorry to say it, I hope I'm not offending anyone here, [LaRouche laughs] but [crosstalk] they've destroyed this country! They've degenerated it to the point that it's at now.

So what I'm asking you is, *how* are we going to get people in Washington, to really focus, and put through legislation, like Glass-Steagall, to really turn the country around?

LaRouche: Actually, the position right now is a little more optimistic than it has been for a very long time. We have some candidates for President, two of them at least, so far,—not Hillary, by the way; she is a real failure when it comes to anything like that. She's absolutely opposed to Glass-Steagall.

But the point is, we have a couple of Presidential candidates, one of whom is more outstanding than the other or others, who actually could be the choice for leadership of the next Presidency. Now, if that were to occur—and I believe it may occur, and I'm certainly in support of its occurring—we do have on hand, the preconditions for dumping Obama, President Obama, and that's a very specific thing.

Now, if you get rid of Obama,—Obama is actually an agent of the British interests. That's what he is. He was created by London, by the British Empire. He was stuck in there; and you had Hillary Clinton trying to run for President, and the British Empire moved in, with agents inside the United States and so forth, who worked with the British, closely, as in California. There was a figure in California who was imported from the British circles in Europe and brought into Hollywood; and he became a leading figure there, for a period. He produced all kinds of things, dirty sex operations, and everything else like that; so we had a factor of corruption, serious corruption.

The Bush family has been a family from its beginning; I'm talking about, first of all, Prescott Bush, who was actually a pro-Hitler prototype! But all the other Bushes that followed from him were kind of stupid. Prescott Bush was clever, a clever thief, a clever everything. But the Bushes otherwise, who got into the Presidency, were all characteristically stupid jerks, to use the right terminology.

But they were useful, for whom? For Wall Street! You put dirty jerks, like the Bushes into the Presidency, what're you going to get? Then they ran out of Bushes. So they got Obama. And Obama's a British agent, pure and simple. Look at the record: The minute he got elected, what did he do? He was the Queen's own maid, or something; he still is! He's a creep, an evil creep! He should never have been the President. It was only a sick government which would allow Obama to become President. There were other sources available: Hillary would have been a much better President, than Obama would ever be. But unfortunately, she became a slave of Obama, and therefore, that option was knocked out.

No, the same thing: We have the means, now. You know, there are people in government, there are four members of the Senate, who acted in concert, on behalf of, in fact, Glass-Steagall. So this is not something that's an impossible dream: It's something that can happen, and must happen.

Now, the problem is right now; Hillary is going to disappear. There's no way, by the discredit she has already placed upon herself, and by the fact that she is a stooge for Obama,—that's been the way she has worked. When she tried to get into the Presidency, and accepted a position under Obama, she thought she was going to be an influence, and she found out she was not going to be. But she didn't resign then, but rather tried to stay on, and she kept keeping in, trying to cater to Obama to keep her position inside the Presidency. And she got cheapened, and cheapened, and cheapened ever more since that time.

Cancel Wall Street

Then she was forced by Obama, to back him up on the willful *assassination* of U.S. government leading

Elizabeth Warren (D-Mass)   *John McCain (R-Ariz)*   *Angus King (I-Maine)*   *Maria Cantwell (D-Wash.)*

Re-instating Glass-Steagall is "not an impossible dream," said LaRouche. Here, the four Senators who initiated the Twenty-First Century Glass-Steagall Act (S. 1709) in the current session of Congress.

agents, and she whimpered around it; *Obama did it!* Obama ordered the killing, of the agents who wiped out American agents, wiped out on the scene! And she knew it, and she fished around with it, which meant, what happened? She became nothing! In the Presidency—nothing!

Yeah, that one thing on the Glass-Steagall issue, that shot her down. And she's spinning downward, all the present time.

So we have some other alternatives: we have members in the Congress, in the Senate, for example, who realize that the Glass-Steagall issue is a *crucial* one, now. That Glass-Steagall has to be uniform, and we have to shut down Wall Street. Wall Street is collectively, absolutely bankrupt! Put it in bankruptcy! Cancel it! All the money of the Wall Street gangsters is worth nothing anyway, in reality: Cancel it! We don't need it! We don't need *that kind* of money!

What we need is the means, to employ people, in employment of various kinds, which are essential to the progress of conditions of mankind's life! And if you support Obama, or support the Bushes before him, you're doing that, you're an idiot or a criminal. A mistake: Cancel them! Get them out of there!

You've got four members of the Senate, who have moved in that direction. I don't know how deep their commitment goes on this thing, but it's something real, it's something important: *Let's get it done.* Now let's work to find a way to get not only a President elected, a new one,—get rid of Obama, get a new President; right? That's what you have to do. And the impeachment of this President, Obama, is a very easy thing to do, once you get at the job properly: You get the right members of the Senate, some of the right members of the House,

you can get the job done. Impeach the bastard!

Q: Well, so you feel optimistic. You feel optimistic that Glass-Steagall will be passed? And you feel optimistic that there are things under way to impeach the President, because he has so many impeachable offenses. He has a long record of impeachable offenses, and still to this moment, he has not been impeached. And people have been calling for his impeachment for, as far as I know, more than two years; probably since he started his second term, at least —

A New Presidency

LaRouche: Yeah.

Q: He can do a lot more damage in the next year. He's got one year left and he can do a lot more damage. So do you feel truly optimistic that things are underway to get this going?

LaRouche: I don't believe in being optimistic, I believe in being successful.

Q: I like that! [applause]

LaRouche: The point is: That's what we have to do, and we can do it. And in Manhattan, right now where you stand, as you stand before me, *that is possible.* Now, the question is, once we recognize the fact that that is *possible*, then we have to do something about it, and we have to be very clear. I think that we can get the motion going. I think it is *already* going. But what the result will be...?

See, what we need, of course, to make it as short as possible, what we need to do, is actually establish a new group of people, who will form the actual Presidency of the United States, as their mission to do, to replace Obama. Get him out of there! That can be done, if you give the people up there a sense of their *confidence* in

The Alternatives: *Bringing Wall Street under control with Glass-Steagall, or thermonuclear war. Here, FDR signing Glass-Steagall into law June 16, 1933, versus what happened after his death—Truman's dropping an atomic bomb on Hiroshima on August 5, 1945.*

National Archives

U.S. National Archives

the fact that you will *get that job done*. Now, we have some members of Congress, of the Senate in particular, who are committed to Glass-Steagall. The implementation of Glass-Steagall will wipe out Wall Street, and the kind of scoundrels in the Senate and elsewhere, who are responsible for these policies.

It takes people to organize people with the guts to do something about it.

Q: You said it, Mr. LaRouche, "guts!" We have a lot of weak ineffectuals in Washington, and we need strong-minded people who are not afraid to stand up to this President.

LaRouche: That's right! And I believe in that doctrine, thoroughly.

Q: Thank you for your time. Thank you. [applause]

The Time is Now

Speed: OK, Lyn, we're now at the conclusion. I'm going to ask you for some summary remarks, but I wanted to remark about the fact that several times today, we heard the idea of "revolution," that we're in revolutionary times, that people are thinking in terms of revolution, and last Monday, in particular, you began talking with our organizers about the notion that real history works by interruptions; it works by disruptions; it doesn't have a smooth tiling; it doesn't have a smooth set of postulates and axioms and so on. So I would just

invite you in summary, to tell us, as you already have done, what you want us to do. But a little bit about this principle of interruption.

LaRouche: Yeah, well, simply, we've got a situation where, if you allowed the current process which has gone on in the United States so far in the Presidency, allow that to continue? First of all, you get two actions: If Obama remains in the Presidency and is not removed from the Presidency, you're looking at a summertime breakout, burst, of thermonuclear warfare, which will probably depopulate most of the human population. That's what we're faced with! That's the fact!

On the other hand, at the same time, even if this wouldn't happen, you would find the worsening conditions of life of the citizen inside the United States, and also in most of Europe, would be terrible, awful. Therefore, the time is up for people who can, to step forward, to get Glass-Steagall in place in the United States, and to take comparable actions and reconstruction in Europe and elsewhere. Without that measure, mankind has a very poor chance of surviving.

So let's just do it! [applause]

Speed: Thank you very much, Lyn. And I'm sure we're going to see you next week. I think most of us are going to be enthusiastic about that proposition!

LaRouche: [laughs] Wunderschön!

Pluto: What Does it Mean?

by Marsha Freeman and Benjamin Deniston

July 26—New Horizons' Pluto flyby has opened our eyes to a surprisingly active and dynamic world—shocking the scientific community. What might we make of these surprises, these anomalies? What are we really looking at?

Following the path created by Nicolaus of Cusa's defining and founding modern science,[1], Johannes Kepler discovered that the Earth was a subsumed member of the higher order harmonic organization of the Solar System.[2] Today we look to a further step along that path, to understand the Solar System as a subsumed feature of an even higher order process, our Galaxy.

This challenge was recently elaborated in the LaRouche PAC Scientific Team Research Report, "Towards a Galactic Science Driver."[3] This galactic perspective points towards a new framework to examine otherwise anomalous or unexpected features of our Solar System, as Pluto has provided the most recent provocations, even though we don't yet really know the meaning of what we've seen, or of the much more we are yet to see of Pluto.

Already, the New Horizons spacecraft has disproven much of accepted knowledge. Pluto, it turns out, is not a cold, distant world so small that its arrested planetary evolution created an inert body, with few distinguishing features. New Horizons has shown us a planet with smooth icy plains and mountains and troughs, indicative of a geologically-active body, and an atmosphere that is evolving and in complex interaction with the solar wind.

It will take more than a year for the complete set of data that is currently stored in the memory of New Horizons to be transmitted to Earth (while New Horizons continues to record and send back more data, as it proceeds still further into the outskirts of the Solar System).

1. Nicholas of Cusa, *De Docta Ignorantia,* 1440.
2. Johannes Kepler, *Harmonices Mundi,* 1619.
3. Benjamin Deniston and Meghan Rouillard, "Towards a Galactic Science Driver," *EIR*, July 17, 2015.

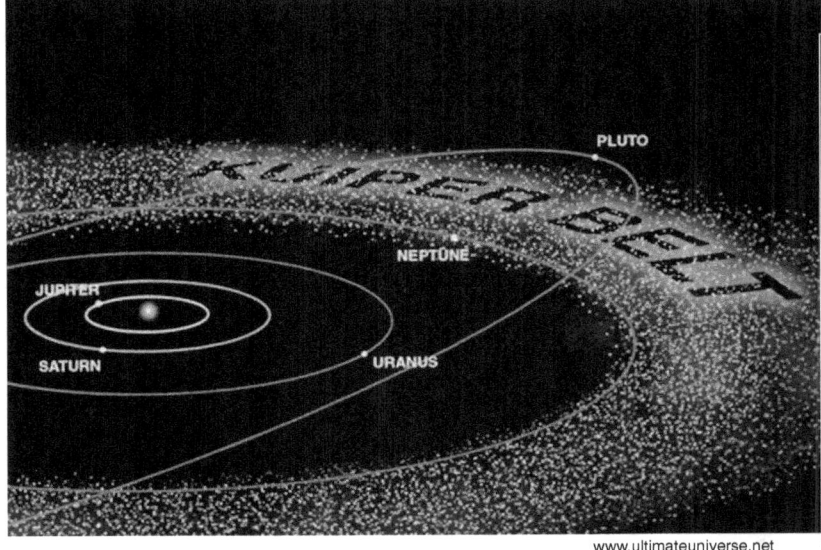

www.ultimateuniverse.net

Pluto's place in the Solar System—and a closeup taken by New Horizons just hours before its closest approach.

NASA/Johns Hopkins University Applied Physics Laboratory/Southwest Research Institute

But already, even with less than 5% of the recorded data now in the hands of scientists, there have been many shocks.

Pluto's Family and Stellar System Structures

Before 1992, scientists conceived of our Solar System as being divided into two regions, one containing the four solid-bodied terrestrial planets (Mercury, Venus, Earth and Mars), and the other, the four gas giants (Jupiter, Saturn, Uranus and Neptune), separated from them by the asteroid belt. Pluto, since its discovery in 1930, was an anomaly—a very small icy body, with a highly-irregular orbit beyond Neptune, which somehow never made it to full planethood.

NASA/Johns Hopkins University Applied Physics Laboratory/Southwest Research Institute

SWAP (Solar Wind Around Pluto instrument) being installed on the New Horizons spacecraft, on March 8, 2006. It will provide scientists with a picture of the character of the solar wind, three billion miles from the Sun, and its interaction with Pluto's atmosphere.

In that year (1992), observational proof was obtained for a theory that Dutch-born astronomer, Gerard Kuiper, had put forward in the 1950s—that beyond the orbit of Neptune, there was a belt of small primitive icy bodies, too small to have coalesced into planets billions of years ago. This stunted evolution, it was proposed, would provide scientists with samples from some of the earliest phases in the development of the Solar System. In 1992, astronomers discovered a small body a billion miles beyond Pluto (named 1992 QB1), and since then, more than 1,000 additional objects have been found, defining what we now call the Kuiper Belt. It has been estimated that there could be over 100,000 bodies larger than 100 kilometers in diameter populating this second belt (tens of times wider and tens to hundreds of times more massive than the asteroid belt).

Pluto is now considered to be the largest representative of this outer system, and many interesting questions come with the study of this often-ignored second belt. For example, scientists are still trying to explain the anomaly of the "Kuiper cliff," the outer edge of the Kuiper belt, where the number of bodies suddenly drops off very rapidly. This sharp outer-edge goes against expectations, and the cause for this Kuiper cliff remains a mystery.

Additionally, our Solar System isn't the only known

stellar system in our galaxy to have a pair of belts. A January 2013 NASA-JPL press release announced the discovery of a warmer inner belt and a cooler outer belt around the relatively young star Vega.[4] As noted in the release, this was actually the second stellar system discovered with similar features, as the star Fomalhaut (also relatively young) was already known to have its own pair of belts. Perhaps most interesting, in all three cases (our Solar System, Vega, and Fomalhaut) the belts have roughly the same relative spacing—with the distance of the outer belt from its star being about ten times the distance of the inner belt.

So Pluto comes to us as a featured part of a rather interesting region of our Solar System.

The Pluto System

Before New Horizons, visual images of Pluto, from ground-based telescopes and the Earth-orbiting Hubble Space Telescope, only revealed a fuzzy ball that is highly reflective, indicating fresh snow, and a surface showing markings in shades of red, perhaps from hydrocarbons. It was known that Pluto has an atmosphere, made up of methane, carbon monoxide, and nitrogen,

---

4. "NASA, ESA Telescopes Find Evidence for Asteroid Belt Around Vega," January 8, 2013.

which exists when Pluto is close to the Sun, but which freezes when Pluto is on its outward path, producing "snow." This lent urgency to the launch of New Horizons, because the 2006 launch meant a 2015 flyby, and by 1989, Pluto's travels in its 248-year orbit had already started it on its path away from the Sun.

Due to its extremely long orbit around the Sun, "the founding fathers had the last opportunity" to study Pluto's atmosphere in 2009, said project scientist Hal Weaver. Pluto's fuzzy visage from afar made it difficult to precisely determine its size, with a round figure used of two-thirds the size of Earth's Moon. It turned out that Pluto, at 1,473 miles in diameter, is a little larger than previously estimated. This change in size means a change in the estimated density of Pluto, indicating a composition consisting of less rock and more ice.

Scientists are at a loss to explain the group of moons that are in Pluto's neighborhood. Charon, the largest of Pluto's five moons, which was discovered in 1978, has half the diameter of Pluto—about equal to the width of Texas—and is the largest moon, relative to its planet, in the Solar System. Pluto and Charon are a double planet, or binary system, as they orbit around a common center of gravity. They are also tidally locked, like the Earth and the Moon, with the same face of Pluto always facing Charon. Charon was known to be covered in water ice, but to have no substantial atmosphere. Two smaller moons, Hydra and Nix, were discovered in 2005 using the Hubble Space Telescope, and after the launch of New Horizons, astronomers found the minuscule Styx and Kerberos.

Signs of Geological Activity

From even a distance of 3.3 million miles, the Pluto that was coming into the view of New Horizon's cameras revealed a body with distinct features, some indicating an active geologic past, or even present.

One of these features is what has been described as a "range of youthful mountains," rising as high as 11,000 feet above the surface. The mountain range was named Norgay Mountains, for Tenzing Norgay, one of

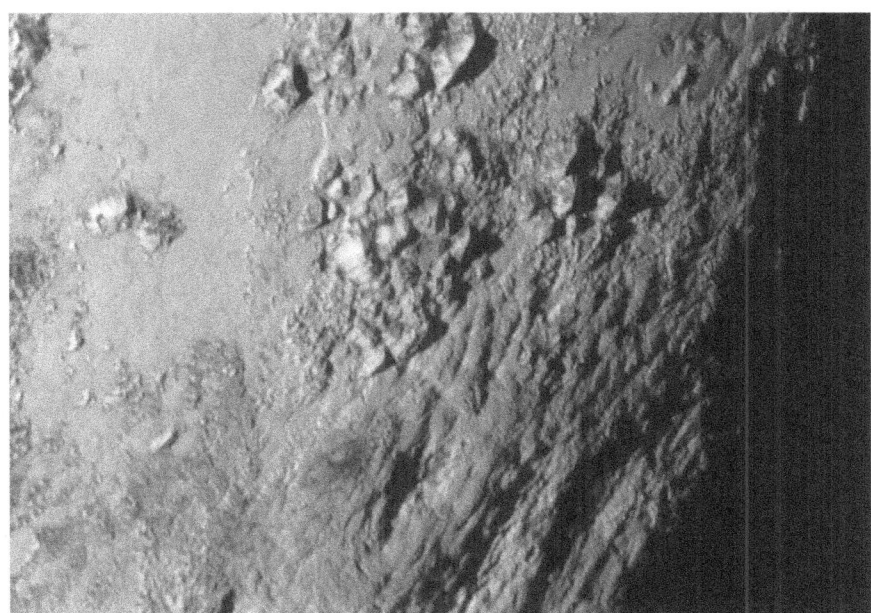

NASA/Johns Hopkins University Applied Physics Laboratory/Southwest Research Institute

These icy mountains of Pluto, observed just before its close encounter on July 14, are very young, an estimated 100 million years old. Scientists propose they may still be forming.

the first people to reach the summit of Mount Everest. "This may cause us to rethink what powers geological activity on many other icy worlds," said science team member John Spencer. Although methane and nitrogen ice cover much of the surface of Pluto, it is believed they would not be strong enough to support the mountains, and that water ice created the peaks.

On July 21, New Horizon scientists released a new image of Pluto's dominant heart-shaped Tombaugh region, named for Pluto's discoverer, which shows a second mountain range bordering the southern end. This second group of mountains is shorter than the Rocky Mountain-sized Norgay range discovered on July 15th, and, at about a half-mile height, is comparable to the eastern U.S. Appalachian Mountains.

In addition to these impressive mountains, photos have also revealed a dramatic contrast in Pluto's terrain. "There is a pronounced difference in texture between the younger, frozen plains to the east and the dark, heavily-cratered terrain to the west," said Jeffrey Moore, who leads the Geology, Geophysics, and Imaging team. "There's a complex interaction going on between the bright and the dark materials, that we're still trying to understand."

These "younger" frozen plains provide a second feature lending strong evidence to the new conclusion that Pluto has been recently—or is even currently—geologically active.

This large smooth, craterless patch has been named "Sputnik plains." The surface "could be a week old, for all we know," said Jeffrey Moore. Scientists could only describe what was presented as "highly complex." Moore quipped at a July 17th briefing, "When I first saw the images of Sputnik plain, I decided I was going to call it 'not easy to explain terrain.'"

More detailed images revealed that Sputnik's icy plain contained a surface that is broken up into segments, shaped like irregular polygons. Some of the segments are bordered by what look like shallow troughs, in a complex geology which cannot yet be explained.

These smooth and uninterrupted features are in marked contrast to other minor bodies which don't have the geological activity needed to smooth out the effects of the regular impacts which come with living in the Solar System. Project scientists explained that Pluto's unblemished plains indicate a young, active surface that could still be changing, due to tectonic activity, or erosion. Dr. Alan Stern, Principal Investigator for the mission, reported that although astronomers have seen other geologically active small icy worlds, these are moons of the giant gas planets, and their geologic activity was explained as a result of tidal heating from the planet.

In Pluto's case, he said, there was no body nearby that could be tugging at Pluto, so geologic activity had to be the result of heat generated internally. One possibility is remnant radioactive material in Pluto, and also Charon, but that would require a much higher concentration than is expected for any other planetary body.

Simply stated, no one expected Pluto to be able to be geologically active, and no one knows why or how it is so.

A Galactic Perspective

It is important to look at Pluto's anomalous activity from the standpoint of the recent research report, "To-

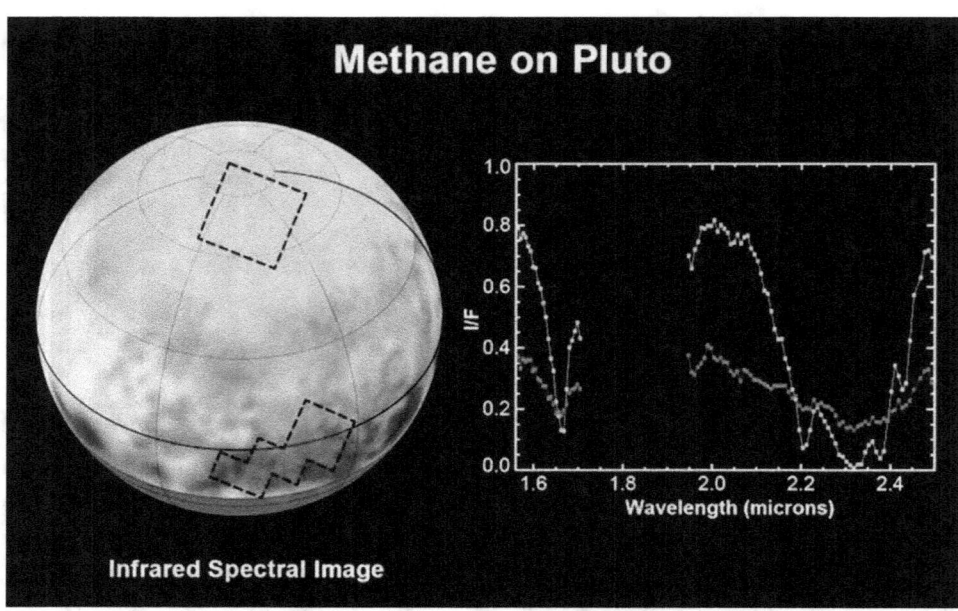

NASA/Johns Hopkins University Applied Physics Laboratory/Southwest Research Institute

Although frozen methane was known to be present on the surface of Pluto, before the arrival of New Horizons, the new data indicate it is not evenly distributed.

wards a Galactic Science Driver."

A common problem permeating science today is the insistence on investigating these questions from the bottom up. It is assumed that we should start from individual bodies, largely governed by their own internal characteristics, and build up larger systems from the additive accumulation of these self-determined parts. However, we can avoid this bottom-up approach with a renewed focus on the Galaxy as the subsuming, higher order process. In this approach we examine activity and changes in the Solar System as potentially expressing the influence of the subsuming Galaxy.

For example, studies have indicated that periods of intense geophysical activity on Earth correspond with the changing relation of the Solar System to the galaxy.[5] We have additional indications that the most recent periods of volcanic activity on the Moon correspond with the most recent periods of intense volcanic activity on Earth—showing us two supposedly independent bodies coming into and out of volcanic activity simultaneously, as if responding to the same external influence.[6]

Pluto doesn't yet give us any answers; indeed, we don't yet really know what we've been looking at.

---

5. For example, see "A Vernadskian Reconsideration of Galactic Cycles and Evolution," in "Toward a Galactic Science-Driver," *EIR*, July 17, 2015.
6 See "Earth-Moon Comparative Planetology," in "Toward a Galactic Science-Driver," *EIR*, July 17, 2015.

LaRouche Wakes Up the Sleepwalkers

July 23—In his July 18 dialogue with the Manhattan Project and subsequently, Lyndon LaRouche has spoken with a new level of frankness on both the depth and the immediacy of the danger facing the world today, and also on the shocking refusal of even most people who consider themselves the most dedicated and the best-informed, to really understand what time it is. We're on the verge of the collapse of the trans-Atlantic system, which can come in various ways. Most of those ways are very, very bad ways: they involve the extermination of most Americans for one thing. But they're not aware of it, and they want to deny that such a thing could exist,—but that's exactly what does exist.

They talk among each other, and they come up with consoling ideas which should not be adopted. We have to take a harder fight on this, because we're in dangerous waters in the short term. These summer months, this very month itself, is a deadly month. People who are trying to get a long-term view of what the future is, are doing worse than wasting time. We need certain actions immediately.

Too many do not understand the issue, because they have too many facts that clutter up their attention. The situation is presently deadly. We're approaching a terminal state of international affairs very rapidly right now. "I know what has to be done," LaRouche said, but he has great difficulty in getting it understood. "We sunk Hillary: one of our members sunk Hillary, by inducing her, in fact, to make a fool of herself. This has gotten things disrupted. But our situation is not such that you could get a deductive insight into the course of history right now. This thing is ready to blow, fully. I'm thinking in terms of days and weeks, at most, before the whole thing comes to a decision. I think right now, the threat is potentially, hopefully, that the British Queen would be thrown out by the British themselves. We're waiting for the effect within a week or so: is the British Monarchy going to collapse globally?"

Of course, we can't say, "What do we bet on?" We have to act to influence the event such that it will be determined, partly, by our influence. But the idea that you can deduce effects in practical ways: forget it, that's gone. What my associates and I do to fight in our organization is indispensable. But the question is getting a clear view of what this is about. Not diminishing things on the horizon; you've got to see the horizon. It may be a big storm coming on. Well, this is not an ordinary storm. It turns out to be something much more forceful.

What we're doing, is often what I'm able to do. That's the problem. On this, the great majority is hopeless. They have no realization of what the reality of things is, right now. They just don't have it. They have specific issues, and they miss the big ones, the ones that are most important. You think you're getting a thundershower; you find out you're getting a tornado. And the good thing is that the British monarchy is on the verge of collapse.

That's the good news. They may escape it, but I doubt it. And it's probable that in two weeks or so, we will get the end of the British Monarchy. But people don't see it. It's coming like a thunderstorm, or like a tornado on the horizon of immediate experience. And the British Monarchy is doing everything to prevent that collapse. But now, the collapse has control of them. It could be two weeks. We don't know, but we know those are the kinds of things we're facing in the next week or so.

We've come to the point: people have been fooling around, "Yes, but; my experience; our experience; this is going to happen; that's not going to happen…" It's nonsense. Because they all believe in statistical methods. And statistical methods are the mark of the idiot. Because the future of mankind lies in the future, not in experience of the past. And the idea of being practical, using statistics, things like that, is what makes people impotent. Makes fools of them.

I gave a lesson over the weekend (July 18), which should be a lesson for them to study. That kind of exposition should be the method; when you try to interpret a couple of facts, as your method of policy-shaping, you're really incompetent; you're pitiful. You have to look at the future; don't rely on statistics; never believe in statistics ever, especially now. People don't realize that what they've been educated to believe in, is actually poisonous and foolish. When I hear the words, "Let's be practical," I say, "Mankind is committing suicide."

Put a cheerful point on it: say, "What we've believed in was all crap; now let's get serious." People speak of the merits of experience. I try to warn them about experience.

People believe, first of all, in statistics. These are forces of demoralization and degeneration which have come in since 1890. The beliefs which have been established under the aegis of that conception, have deluded people to where they have no intelligence of the future. They think of statistics, and people who believe in statistical evidence are just fools. They'll be caught up by the first storm which catches them. They don't see the future. At best, they see what they have experienced in the immediate past, or what they think might be the immediate future. It's just gibberish. Just think of everything printed in newspapers. It's absolutely incompetent; it's a fraud.

They say, "We need more information." What they need is to get rid of some of the information which is fraudulent information. It's much easier to pick up fraudulent information supplied to you, than it is to discover the truth, which always lies in the future. And you know that the U.S. population today has almost no conception of the future, of an actual future of mankind, none. Their future is what they hope or expect for themselves, in the immediate period, their ambitions and their fears. But they don't have a scientific outlook, because they're all practical people. And practical people are stupid people, because they're all going from deduction, deduction from experience. And that's the greatest threat to the human race, of foolishness, which is sort of a global disease.

We tend to have delusions, we believe in things, we try to console ourselves. I have a different life. I worry about different things. I see the things which preoccupy most others, but they're not the major things. Something immediate, something unsettling is seen, but the sight of the process is lost. We just have to improve our diagnoses of things. Be less tempted to draw conclusions from recent or side experiences. We're on the edge of the self-extermination of the human species; in the larger sense, that's the problem. But people are so much concerned about other matters, which to them are a priority, that they overlook the most important things concerning the existence of the human species. And there are some people who get onto these ideas, but then the overwhelming popular opinion goes against them. If you eliminated all the Wall Street people from the equation, you could probably get a good insight into the matter.

I have to fight another day, because I know, most of us so far, are still swallowed by follies. We've made too many mistakes, in effect. Too many false values. And a lot of bad misinformation.

We're on the edge, and if we continue the way we're going, we're going to go over the edge, because, the belief in the statistical outlook on life is the most poisonous and destructive thing imaginable. When someone says, "Be practical," you should shoot them, as the most merciful act for them.

People tend to learn from experience, but they don't see what they have not yet experienced. They believe too much in experience to date. Our society is not organized,—take the U.S.,—in the way which is necessary for the well-being of our people; they have delusions. You can pick up what the delusions are from almost any street-corner. They're running around with delusions. The economy is disintegrating at a rapid rate. The condition of life of our citizens is plummeting. The prospects of our survival are plummeting. And society does not respond to attacking those threats. They want to solidify their existing opinions, their existing prospects as they see them. They're ignorant of the truth of the situation. They're totally disarmed. A thunderstorm could come along, and sweep them all off the map of the earth. Their eyes or their opinions are gazing in the wrong direction. They're not paying attention to reality. They're paying attention to their wishful fantasies, or their meaningless fears.

Go Where Mankind Has Never Gone Before!

John Ascher:: I want to welcome everyone back. This is John Ascher in Leesburg, Virginia, and we are here for our tenth Fireside Chat with Lyndon LaRouche, here on the 23rd of July, 2015.

Well, I think what I'm going to do at this point, as we're getting our other speaker on, I'm going to get Tony Papert on here to begin by reading a special message which has been formulated by a discussion between him and Mr. LaRouche earlier today, which will be an editorial in the upcoming issue of *Executive Intelligence Review*.

Tony Papert: It's titled, "LaRouche Wakes Up the Sleepwalkers": [reads statement appearing on page 28]

John Ascher: Thank you, Tony.

Lyn, are you there? Lyn, do you have anything you'd like to add to the statement that Tony just read before we get on to the questions?

Lyndon LaRouche: Just as a matter of following up on immediately what Tony reported. The point is, we're living in a society where most people have beliefs, and the beliefs are based on certain conditioning, but they always really are thinking, either in the fantasy of the future, or try to rely upon the past as the substitute for future, for understanding the future. And the problem is, how do you get people to get free of that?

What I'm doing with that, of course, I'm getting rather ruthless in one sense, on what we do on Saturday in Manhattan, which is one of the things I work on. And since that time, since last weekend when I made my report on that subject then, I've taken a tougher position on this thing, because I realize that most of our citizens, who think they have knowledge, don't, because of the idea of being practical; or the idea of being deductive.

And all humanity, and the very characteristic of humanity, good humanity, is to see a future, which mankind had never experienced before. That's the characteristic of mankind. In animals, it's different. The animal life generally bases its very existence, on a certainty of what their species, in the course of life, had presented them with. They never see the future; the future may hit them, but they don't see it as the future. They don't see it as a new quality, a change of life, to a better form of life. Animals cannot do that. They cannot see that. Only human beings have the power to see the future. No animal can see the future, only human beings. And unfortunately, only the few

CNTV

The characteristic of mankind is to see the future,—and no nation is exhibiting this characteristic more than China. Here, China's Yutu (Jade Rabbit) orbiter shown in close-up after its arrival on the Moon on December 14, 2013.

human beings, who understand what the meaning of the future is.

We Don't Have Science Any More

And therefore, today, I find most of what I have to do, is I have to correct the mistakes of popular opinion, correct the error in which people put confidence in popular opinion. And if they thought carefully, if they look at one thing—let's look from the beginning of this cycle. Now, the cycle begins at the last decade before the Twentieth Century, about ten years before the last time. And since that time, mankind has drifted more and more, into assuming that what was happening then, at a moment, will be what's going to happen the day after, or two days after or something like that.

We don't have science any more; we have mathematics. Mathematics is the substitute, officially since the Twentieth Century, as a replacement, for science. In other words, mathematics and the methods of mathematics, are treated as a *mere substitute*, for what is actually science, and that means the very idea of understanding the future. But remember, mankind is the only species which is truly, intrinsically creative by its nature. No form of mere animal life, is capable of understanding the future. And most people, today, act like animals do, when they call that *"being practical"*.

So that's what we've got to overcome.

Ascher: Okay, with that, I'm going to turn on our button to get people into line. [Describes protocol for submitting questions by phone or YouTube, Facebook, and Twitter.]

Q: Yes, this is R__ from Mansfield, Mass. I'm a former resident of New Hampshire, like Lyndon. I grew up in Franklin, New Hampshire; went to school in Concord, and then went to Northeastern University, back in the '70s to get my bachelor's and master's degree.

I've got a question. I'm a little confused as to who's pulling the strings? Is it the British Royal Family, or is it the Rothschild bank holding company which produces the fiat money, propping them and supporting the Western financial system? Because that's sort of issue #1.

Issue #2 is, the minions of the Rothschild banking system and the British Royal Family, their minions including all of these conservative think tanks, Heritage Foundation, Tavistock Institute, and the Council on Foreign Relations, these folks are borrowing money at 25 basis points from the Federal Reserve, and now acquiring American corporations with fiat money, which

is not based on anything, which is merely counterfeited. Where I grew up in New Hampshire, quantitative easing was another word for counterfeiting. [LaRouche laughs]

I'm going to hang up and listen to Mr. LaRouche's answer. Thank you, very much.

A History of Swindle

LaRouche: OK. Well, I think the thing can be simplified. First of all, what there has been is a history of swindle, in terms of the United States itself. We had a great President, Washington; he was advised and was made by a genius [Alexander Hamilton], by a great scientist who designed the economic policy of the United States. Then the great scientist, who had backed up George Washington as President, was assassinated, of course. And what happened after that, we had a second President of the United States, who was not a bad person, but was not a particularly competent person for the kind of problems that the creation of the new United States demanded.

After that, we had a third President, who was a *rotten*, pro-slave, in a slavery-promoting organization; and we had a series of Presidents after that, who were all pretty much in the same general line. We had a President who was very great [John Quincy Adams]; he served one term and was bounced out of that office and bounced into the Congress. He actually contributed greatly to what happened after that, our success with Abraham Lincoln; he promoted that. And we had a period of good things, a short period of good things.

Then we had the usual bouncing back and forth between good Presidents and bad ones, in terms of general characteristic.

Great Presidents Assassinated

Then we closed out into the Twentieth Century, by assassinating one of the best Presidents, and we brought in a guy for two terms in office, who was damned evil. And most of our Presidents tended to be rather evil, at least in that process. So what has happened is, the pragmatic attitude which is borrowed from the British Empire, has been dominant, during most of the periods of the Twentieth Century. We've had only a few Presidents, Franklin Roosevelt particularly, only a few Presidents who were either well-meaning, or actually great. And the great ones usually got assassinated, or something like that. And that's our condition now.

In that sense, we actually have been under the control of the British Empire. But, however, something interesting is happening. We're on the edge of the point that the British Empire is about to be shut down. Now, I can't give you the exact date, when that is going to occur. I can say that the first steps, for shutting down the British Monarchy are already in process.

Now, if we can get that done soon enough, we can probably avoid a global thermonuclear war. The danger of thermonuclear war comes, especially from President Obama: If President Obama is not removed, fairly soon, or the conditions around him not are fixed to steer a solution, we're all going to get into a thermonuclear war. And a thermonuclear war, which is the only kind of general war that the United States can ever expect, would be almost the extermination of the human species, in a very short number of hours!

Because once the United States government, under Obama, were to launch what Obama intends to do, and he's made it very clear that's what he intends to do, is to actually start a thermonuclear war against Russia. Now, Russia has a tremendous capability in terms of military operations. So, for the United States' Obama to get into that kind of a fix, is by itself, a cause for the virtual extermination of the human species, in a very short time. So we're on that point.

Now, I'm working on these kinds of things, and with circles which are also working on these kinds of things. But we have *not*,—for most of the existence of our nation, for most of our republic's existence, we've had relatively few Presidents who were not tragedies or outright crooks. And that's become like the case: the Bush family—crooks; Obama—crook. And this comprises eight years each of these two Presidencies, virtually, that alone.

Muster for Something New

And look at the conditions of life of our people, look at the degeneration of the conditions of life of our

EIRNS

Mastery of the principles of Classical musical composition, and performance, are the foundation of successful moral development of the individual. Here, LaRouche PAC leader Diane Sare conducts her Manhattan chorus at a Schiller Institute event on November 23, 2014.

people. Look at the misery they're going through. Now, you've got a Pope, who's a British agent; he's actually a creation of the British agent [Hans Joachim (John) Schellnhuber], and they're trying to destroy the human race by reducing the number of people.

We have a governor in California. Now, the father of that governor, the father was not a bad guy. They're both Catholics from California, but the father was not a bad guy at all; matter of fact, he did a lot of good things. But the present governor of California, is an absolute evil disaster! Now, why's he an evil disaster? Because he was raised to be an evil disaster, and there are some ways you can explain how that happened, but that's what happened.

So this is the problem: We're on the point that unless we can muster ourselves, not to be practical, not to eliminate mistakes, but to actually begin something *new*, not something that was old; something new that corresponds to the future of mankind, and that's what I'm dedicated to.

Q: Hi, this is Lynn Yen from New York. I'm the Executive Director of the Foundation for the Revival of Classical Culture [FFTROCC]. Lyn, I have a question, which is that we're about to start on this upcoming Monday, our 2015 Music and Science program.

We have something like twenty young people between the ages of 12 to 17. And they're going to have their music in the morning; they're going to do chorus with the emphasis on polyphony. And I would like for them to have—in the course of the five weeks of studies—a grounding of what the scientific basis, for example, of the proper tuning is. But more than that, also to have a science of actually their own history, their own sense of humanity.

Because today, as we all know, the atmosphere of violence in America, and apathy and lack of humanity in America, is kind of like in Johannes Kepler's time. And our young people represent the hope of the future of mankind, and I want these young people to actually see the hope in their own lives through the knowledge that they can acquire through things like—I would like for them, for example, to really have a grounding in Kepler's work, in Kepler's music of the spheres; and various other topics, such as American history which they never learn properly in school.

And I was wondering if you can come in on that and help me with that?

Between the Notes

LaRouche: OK, fine. I think the first thing we need, is you need people who are experts in the sense of their own development, in the principles of Classical musical composition. This means, essentially, the people who are going to go through the experience, which follows the trail from the founding of Johann Sebastian Bach. Because Bach introduced a principle of composition and elaborated it somewhat in the course of his lifetime as well.

Then he had followers, such as Mozart, and Mozart was an absolute genius; and Beethoven, an absolute genius. And you had followers of these geniuses who set forth a principle of musical composition, and that principle, while it may seem complicated to some people, is actually the foundation, of all competent success in the moral development which is a necessary development of the human individual; a moral development in which the student, as being educated in music and practicing music, first of all, has the idea of locating the voice.

In other words, if the person tries to sing the voice on the idea of trying to sing as such, they'll often fail, and they'll get into bad habits that will lead into confusion. But what has happened in the course of history, from Bach into the beginning of the Nineteenth and Twentieth Century,—the last great man was, essentially, at one point was Brahms. Then you had a few people who spilled over into the Twentieth Century,

and typical of course, was Furtwängler. And Furtwängler's role is typified by one example which any teacher of singing should have as a basis for approaching students—any kind of students at all ages.

And the placement of the voice is what the question is: Because the mistake that's made, which is destructive, is when you assume that the tone that you're singing, that is the indicated tone, when you base yourself on that, you get into a trap. Because Classical musical composition is always based *between the notes*: That's the formal expression, *"between the notes,"* not *on* the notes. The notes are there, but it's the motion *between* the notes, which defines the kind of composition which is intended by all the great composers and the great performing artists.

And therefore, what you want to have, is you want to have the moral benefit, and it's a real psychological benefit, from throwing your voice out in order to play, instead of being stuck in the voice. It's a question of the movement of the voice from *one note* going between the next note. And the way this thing works, it has been the basis of all great musical composition since the original design of modern music by Bach. And all this thing, up through the achievement, in particular, of Furtwängler.

Because Furtwängler—they had a little problem they had to deal with: The problem was, how does the Ninth Symphony of Schubert function? Now the score of Schubert's Ninth Symphony was known to anyone who was a professional musician during that period. But, how is it supposed to work? And what happened is that Furtwängler reminded people, that the principle of composition did not lie *on* the note; it lay *between* the notes. In other words, the motion, of the notes, between the notes as a series, is the principle of actual Classical musical composition.

Now, this is not just Classical musical composition as some kind of a system. It is the very principle in which the student, when brought into that realm, when they begin to see themselves and what their voice means, they realize that the important place is not the sound of the voice; it is the *between* the notes: That is, you have a tone, and you have a tone on the other side; and in that process, that succession of tones in that order, provides what's called "between the notes."

The ability to get even simply trained children, into getting the idea of singing between the notes, is the most important moral and psychological step we can do, and should begin very soon, in the early stages of trying to help the student of music, help them see what the meaning is of between the notes. And when you get them to that point, you put them on the road for, really, an insight into the real meaning, of Classical artistic composition.

And that's what we want to do: We want to make little geniuses, out of little people.

What Is a 'Godly' Approach?

Ascher: Well, that's wonderful.

Q: Lyn, I have a question here from someone listening via YouTube, which is somewhat in a similar direction, not precisely on music but I'm going to read this. It's from N__ from Las Vegas. And here is his question:

"Sir, I believe the only chance we have as a nation to lead the world towards a better world, is to gather a sizeable group of enlightened people, who will be listened to by the weight of their Godly character. Is this a workable plan, to effect the movement of the masses to something that will turn us towards positivity? Thanks, N__" That's his question.

LaRouche: OK! Well, the problem is, what do you mean by that? I mean, you mention a "Godly approach" but what is a Godly approach? Now, I have a very good, clear idea of what I mean by that, and I would say this thing about music we just talked about, you know, children's training in music, I think is pretty much an entry point to knowing what a "Godly approach" would be.

In other words, if you can get people to locate themselves, in a sense of the beauty which is found "between the notes" in Classical musical singing training, that the person, you know, is not banging it all out on a guitar or something like that; they're not noisemakers. But many people today—you know, we have very few people who are actually musicians any more. We have people who are called musicians, but they really aren't musicians; they're clowns. They really are clowns—and they're bad clowns with bad tastes!

So what we want to do: you want to take a principle as such, Classical music, according to discipline, and when you actually achieve the ability, to lead young

EIRNS/Stuart Lewis

"When you get the student to sing a beautiful voice—even for a little chld, a beautiful voice which lies between the notes—that's when you've succeeded." Here, the famous Thomanerchor boys' choir [founded 1212] from Leipzig, Germany singing at a Schiller Institute-sponsored concert in Washington, D.C. on February 7, 1998.

children, at those ages, to get into the place where they recognize, suddenly, they come to a point of convergence, shall we say, where they actually understand the importance of "singing between the notes." In other words, the idea, in all great music, is that it is not the note which makes the music; it is the voice, which is placed between the notes in a very specific kind of way. And that is what brings the student of music into the point that they located, very importantly, the placement of their voice between the notes.

That is, when they're singing *a* note, on a note, and they go out from that to another step, they come to a point where they are between the notes. And it's when they come to that between-the-note thing, that they reassess what they think is the note, and they want to place it, so that the sound of the note itself becomes something in between, which then inspires the expression of the next note assigned.

And when you get the student to sing a beautiful voice, even for a little child, a beautiful voice which lies between the notes, that's when you've succeeded.

Cusa's Mission

Ascher: Well, I have question also sent in, Lyn, from YouTube, which is in a similar direction, so I think I'll just read this to you right now.

Q: It's from a gentleman named T__, from Texas.

And what he said is, "Lyn, how should I understand the concept of Creation, that is God, because I think it's a little hard to understand this Creation concept?" He said, "There are various interpretations of it."

LaRouche: Well, I would say that the argument of Nicolaus of Cusa probably stands till today, as a good point of reference for defining what must be the case. Now, the point is, if you really get the chance to expose yourself to Nicolaus of Cusa, who is actually, really the founder of a whole doctrine of Christian belief, which is also a reflection which also took into account the ancient Greek. . . .

Just let me for a minute explain: When Nicolaus of Cusa, who was actually one of the great leaders of the Christian church in his lifetime, had taken a visit to the archives of ancient Greece, and when he got there, he was somewhat disappointed on one account. He could get the writings of the great Greek thinkers, but they weren't practicing those great thinking processes right then! And so, Nicolaus of Cusa made a turn in his perspective of what he could do, and he defined a new view of the approach of mankind, to mankind's Godly intention.

Now, this becomes problematic, because what happened at the beginning of the following century, after the [Fifteenth] Century in which Nicolaus had lived, the Catholic Church was a *monster*, in the main! An absolute monster! You know, killing people, burning them alive, all these kinds of things, these horror shows, and that was somehow ameliorated later, temporarily, and we went into a new period, which was the period of Nicolaus of Cusa's follower, Johannes Kepler, for example, and also some great people in that period, from the death of Kepler into the middle of the founding of the U.S. society.

The 'God' Principle

And so, there is an actual history, which does correspond to mankind's view of what a deity is. Now, a deity is not an object, because a deity, a true deity, is one that has been creating the universe; not something that is out there inventing something, but has been creating the universe, by leading mankind to a higher level of insight, a higher level of mission.

Like, for example, now: We have a couple of points which are really pedagogical. One, Nicolaus of Cusa, followed by what? By the founder of the discovery of the Solar System, the first man who discovered the Solar System: Kepler. Then you had a whole period of people who were great geniuses, and they are the ones who supplied the kickoff for the American Revolution.

So, that's the way to look at it. There is a fundamental way, not where you say, God is going to come down and throw some writing in front of you or something like that; it doesn't happen. When we're talking about God, it should mean the Creator of the Universe. Or the Creative Power of the Universe, in the Universe. And that's what Christianity, in particular, should mean. God is not something which is controlled by the present. What we should mean by God, is the existence of a powerful force which is humanoid in its intention, which lifts mankind out of all kinds of despair and failures, to realize that mankind must become, something always between, [better] than his present generation had been, and that should be followed by something *higher*, in a next generation.

And that's the meaning of the God principle: There's a principle in the universe, which is part of the power of the universe, and that mankind is privileged, against all other living species, to participate in the intention of that great Creator.

The Meaning of Your Life

Q: Hi, this is K__ from Massachusetts. Hi, Mr. LaRouche. I try to go out, and depending upon the weather, but it's usually pretty nice, and you know, start a conversation with people regarding what's going on in the world. And they'll say, "Oh, no, that can't be. I saw O'Reilly, or whatever his name is, on Fox News, and he didn't say anything about that! So you can't be right." Or, "I saw this in the newspaper—Putin is an animal, he's a dictator! He's not good!" And I'll say, "He's a good man and he loves his country, and wants to protect his people." I said, "Where did you get that information?"

"Well, I, I—it was in the newspaper." I said, "What're you doing reading the newspaper? Get rid of your TV, and stop your subscription to the newspaper, 'cause all you're getting is lies."

LaRouche: Yeah, yeah. Well, I think, you know, the whole problem is: look, everyone's going to die. Every human being is going to die. I'm sort of a holdout, in the 94 years of age, so I'm sort of a holdout; and there are a few people older than I am who are still functional. I'm fortunately functional. Most people who are alive, who have been alive, are either dead, or incapacitated. So I'm one of those lucky people who still has the prowess

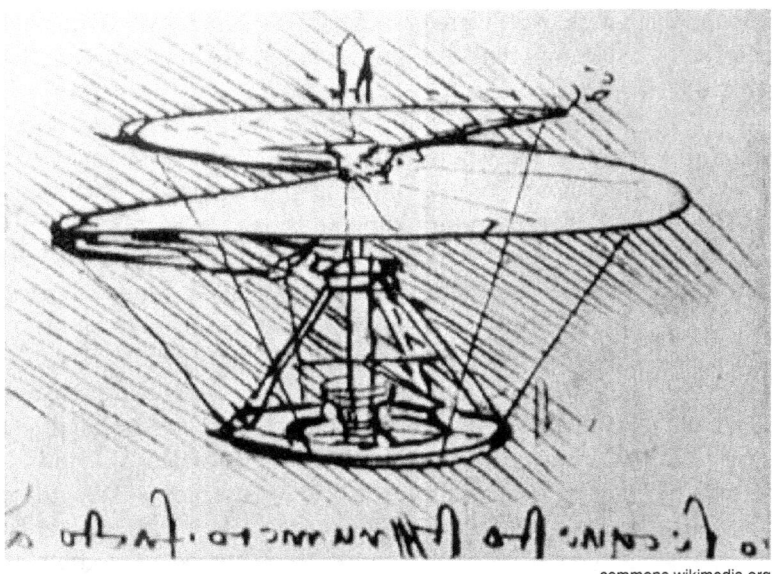

commons.wikimedia.org

Mankind's discoveries, passed on to future generations, make him an "immortal institution," as LaRouche put it. Here, one of legendary discoverer Leonardo da Vinci's scientific studies for flight—his vision of a helicopter, done in the Fifteenth Century.

to do a few things, and I am determined not to waste my time on that subject.

But the point is, we have to realize, as I said before, just in the previous question that came up: What mankind has to do, is, first of all, accept the fact, of the lack of immortality of mankind as a living being. Everyone human is going to die, sooner or later. The question is, what's the meaning of their life? Does the meaning of their life lie in something they did before they died? Or does the meaning of their life mean, more precisely, that they are going to develop themselves, in order to achieve things for mankind, which mankind has never really accomplished before? Or will fix up and repair what was neglected, earlier?

So mankind has to be an immortal institution, in which the progress of mankind, from a lesser degree of knowledge, is passed on to a higher degree of knowledge. For example, now, at first we knew something about Earth; then we began to discover things beyond Earth, as processes; then we began to discover more things, We had scientific discoveries, actually physical scientific discoveries, new ones. And we had a great zest, a great insight into still higher aptitudes of physical scientific creativity, great artistic composition: like the great artistic composition which started with Bach, and that led to a set of developments in the course of those two centuries, which led mankind to a

higher achievement, a higher moral achievement.

Mankind Has a Mission

And then, when the Twentieth Century came in, then, the musical value, and the moral characteristics of the trans-Atlantic community *degenerated*. And it's been degenerating ever since, in general.

So the problem is, mankind has a mission. The mission is not that we're all going to die, but we are all going to die. The question is, what are we going to create, out of our living processes? And what's our vision of that? That it means that we are being a creative force in ourselves; that whatever we are, we are giving something to the future of mankind which mankind would never have discovered before without our intervention. And that's what we should be basing ourselves on.

We are going to die, all of us are going to die, mortally. But we need not die, in a sense of having contributed something, in the course of our life, to bring mankind to a higher level of existence and knowledge. That's the way it has to be: There is no alternative to that. That's the only reality, that mankind has the power to express.

Ascher: Well, Lyn, I will say, there's a certain degree of being bombarded with questions here related to the Presidential election, so I'm going kind of combine two questions that I've gotten from folks that are listening via YouTube.

Q: One is from J__ from Minnesota; the other is T__ from Virginia. And one of them is basically citing his view that the two party system is a criminal enterprise, and isn't having a third party a legitimate idea?

T__ cites the fact that in the past our movement had run many, many individuals for political office, alongside of yourself, Lyn, when you were running for President, and asking can't we once again run a lot of people for office?

What I've Been Fighting For

LaRouche: OK. I don't think the multiplicity of individuals is going to do that job. My experience tells me, no, that doesn't work that way! It can work that way; we had in a certain point in my own experience, my own leadership with the organization, before I was put in the hoosegow by the Bush family, that there were changes that were made. And when I was put in the hoosegow for a period of time, even though I got out of there and was doing all kinds of things in all parts of the world, even after then. You know, going into other parts of the planet and so forth.

But the point of this thing is, what's important is that we question the failure of mankind today. In other words, what's wrong with the United States? What's wrong with Western Europe, in particular? The trans-Atlantic region, what's wrong with it? What's rotten about it?

Well, I could tell you that my experience, is that beginning, actually from the last decade of the Nineteenth Century, that the United States itself, and also Europe, has been in a constant drift into degeneration. Now, the wars that broke out, and if you look at the history, since the late Nineteenth Century, you find that there's a perpetual degeneration, with some exceptions, since the 1890s.

The good one [William McKinley], was a great President, who was assassinated, before he could live out his life. We had a President who had two terms, and he was an evil fellow; we had some people who were evil fellows, and another generation, evil fellows.

Then we had Franklin Roosevelt. And Roosevelt was a genius, a man of great courage, a man of great insight, a man of great accomplishment. Then we had replacements, in which the FBI went into a degeneration phase; that was bad. Look at their destruction in that whole period! Destruction. And when I got to the point where I got into doing something, about 1970-'71, I busted out and created a new organization. And in that process, by the end of the century, that, with the oncoming onset of the next President, that I was promoted; I was actually a leading figure of the government of that period.

Then I was shut down by the Bush family crowd, and put in the jug for a while just to get rid of me. Then I bounced back and did some more things which were notable, always fighting against these kinds of things and making some successes.

But the essential achievement that I made was the continued fighting for what I knew had to be done. But what I was fighting *for*, was also what I was fighting against; like the degeneration of the Bush family under the Presidency. The deep degeneration of Obama, the Obama Administration, and things like that. *These have all been evil, pure evil!* The Bush family has been a force of evil in the history of the United States.

And Obama, the same thing: Obama is bringing mankind to the brink of thermonuclear war, and that thermonuclear war, if launched under Obama now, during this summertime, would mean the probable extinction of most of the human species.

So those are the real issues we face. Their facts, their considerations, their understanding, for people who understand it, who understand history, the remedies are understandable—at least by some people. And if those "some people" are permitted to show what they *do* know for practice, then we can do a pretty good job.

No Monopoly on History

Q: Good evening, this is R__ from Brooklyn. And the earlier comment by Tony when he was doing the speech earlier on what's going to be in *EIR*, the inaccuracy of the statistics, when I start talking to people, and they ask for "facts," and they ask for this and that, and I tell them some of the facts, it's very difficult for them to comprehend just how the statistics are being gerrymandered, rigged and interpreted.

The governor of California, who you've correctly stated is evil, stated when he was asked how many people were eligible for certain benefits under the new health care system, that there was 800,000 who were homeless, etc. And then, his staff got their act together, and they found out that the state had 2.5 million homeless! This is quite a difference.

What sort of tools can we use to try to wake people up when we talk to them; and when we deal with people, and try to get around this huge, huge lie that they've put in place?

LaRouche: I'll say one thing, which is really the essence of the matter: "They"—the so-called "they"—do not have a monopoly on the shaping of history. And I know that. I know that from experience. And what I've known includes a lot of things where I was set back; but I'm a stubborn cuss, and I tend to not pay much attention to being ordered to drop my account on this thing.

If we actually mobilize a significant minority of the people, who are intelligent people, some of them in the Congress, some of them in related positions, some of them in practices of all kinds, moral practices, scientific practices,—the scientific practice, of course, is poorer today than it ever was before hand; science is almost nonexistent. But there are some people who do understand something about science.

Crush the British Empire

But we also have to see,—look at our situation inside the United States. Look at China: Now, if you look at China now, —China, of course, has always been China, but it's been sometimes stronger in its accomplishment, and sometimes weaker in its accomplishment. We have India: India's going through a kind of a new Renaissance, a new stage of development, which many of us,—like, I was very close to Indira Gandhi and to that whole group; and she was assassinated by the British system. They killed her because she was too successful. And we were close to her. So we have these setbacks of this type. But then, you know, what happens, is, you find in the history of this matter, there are certain kind of revolutions, sort of counter-revolutions against these setbacks.

And this is happening now. Egypt has made a revolution; it doesn't mean it's a perfect revolution, or perfectly successful, but it's a good revolution. And in South America, there are nations which have made *good* revolutions in terms of their development. And so forth and so on.

So what we're trying to do, is to take the evil that we're fighting against, mainly, chiefly the British Empire, that is, the British Royal Family which is not really a human family, but it is something, some kind of creature. Anyway, they're Nazis. I mean the thing is out now: the British Royal Family are a pack of Nazis, and the people in Britain who know this stuff, *know* they're a bunch of Nazis. The Irish know they're Nazis, the Scots know they're Nazis, and many of the English know they're Nazis. And we're on the point, right now, at this moment, where the British Monarchy, the British Empire, is about to be shut down! And the chances are that it's going to be shut down: It may not be next week, but it may be the week after that.

Hillary is Disqualified

And that may be in time to prevent President Obama, who's a stooge of the British Queen and has been from the beginning; if they take them out of business, and put

en.wikipedia. org

Hillary Clinton's capitulation to Barack Obama has broken her spirit, and her Presidential prospects. Here, Secretary of State Clinton confers with Obama in Phnom Penh, Cambodia during a November 2012 trip.

some of our people in business with this new election campaign coming up now, I think the new election options which are coming up now, include some people who are qualified to become President. You have different kinds of people, different people, but if you pull that thing together, you could pull together a Presiden*cy*, not just a President, but a Presiden*cy*: That is a team of people built around, a particular President, which is assigned itself, or does assign itself to take over many different kinds of differentiated tasks which the United States' people need urgently, now. And that's the best way to look at it.

Q: [Ascher] Well, Lyn, I just got an email from my wife Rochelle Ascher, who just indicated that when it comes to the Presidency, which we partly helped to shape with the question from Daniel Burke last Monday to Hillary Clinton, this is reverberating still today. Apparently, Hillary Clinton stuck her head further somewhere in the wrong location today: In South Carolina, she was again asked about Glass-Steagall, and said once again that this would actually be a "mistake."

So I think that the coverage of this indicates how O'Malley, who I think you were just referring to some degree to Martin O'Malley, has really, including today, really hit very, very hard on Glass-Steagall. So we've definitely succeeded in getting this question to the forefront of the Presidential elections already this year, and I think that's very important.

LaRouche:: Yeah, the important thing to think, is think about how Hillary's finished. That she is by all intents and purposes finished. And what's happened to her, here she's actually been prompted and backed up by Obama.

She worked for Obama for a while, which I told her was a mistake, and other people told her was a mistake; and then she was crushed by Obama, because he's a real beast. I mean, he's the worst kind of animal you ever want to talk about. So she was broken. And she left the office that she'd had then under Obama, and she walked out of that. Then she went to work *under* Obama to set up a Presidential candidacy, contrary to everything that I would have wanted, and many other people would have wanted.

She's Not Going to Come Back

So she's really not a factor any more. Because, how'd that happen? Because one of our associates, who was auditing her address in New York City, waited until near the end of her address, and then said, "What about Glass-Steagall?" Now, what happened was, as an immediate result of that, you had all these reporters and so forth who were swarming around this thing, and they suddenly went to work and exposed the whole thing. And she refused to say anything, at that point, on Glass-Steagall! She has said nothing about Glass-Steagall, except to denounce it as she has done again.

Now, on this basis, *she's finished*. There's no way she's going to climb back into the Presidency by her campaign: She's disqualified, permanently! Because she committed a fraud and she got caught in public, and suddenly all these reporters who were coming to witness what she was doing in that speech, picked up immediately on that, and she's wiped out now! She's still running around, she still has backing from certain sources; teams of people still trying to resurrect her. But the point is, her policies are totally *against* the most vital interests of the citizens of the United States. She's proposing to follow through on the Obama policy! Or a branch of the Obama policy; she's still a slave of Obama, in fact.

And she's *not* going to come back, because any of the people who are candidates for leadership in the United States government, honest people, including four members of the Senate now, and they are looking in that direction. Other people are going to be moving more and more in that direction. So, she is finished.

She can do nothing good, because what she's doing is a fraud; it's a fraud against the people. But it's a transparent fraud, and by a good accident, she launched the announcement of her campaign by actually crushing the idea of Glass-Steagall, which she's done ever since then. So she's lost it. She's sung the song which throws her out of the Presidency.

Q: Hello, this is S__ from Riverside, and we haven't heard much about Ukraine lately, and I'm wondering if there's still going to be a provocation; if they're still going to be used as a provocation. And what's going on there, anyhow?

Get Rid of the Statisticians

LaRouche:: Well, the whole thing is tied in with the whole complex process. First of all, the issue on the table right now is the effort to dump the Queen of England. And as a matter of fact, to dump the entire British family, and their attachments. That's on the agenda now. It is not absolutely secure that that's going to happen, but everything now shows that there's a very strong trend, to macerate the British Royal Family. Besides, both of them are a little bit beyond, shall we say, the thinking stage, and they're just actors. And they're all Nazis, you know. All of them, all of the British leaders are Nazis, and that whole story is pouring out now, not only in Britain, it's pouring out all over the world! You know the British Royal Family is a pack of Nazis— oh, news? Well, where were you for the last 50 years?

So I think that's the factor you want to hear about. And the point is, what we have to do is understand what the task is, to get the job done. Let me give you what the problem is: People say, that we use statistics to define where the future is going. Well, that is the most stupid thing that anybody ever suggested; the most stupid thing that ever happened was being "practical." And being practical in terms of what popular opinion thinks is practical. That really is idiocy, and that's what's killed most people; they try to be practical.

Now, the point is, they believe that statistics does it; it means they use mathematics. Well, mathematics is not science, contrary to popular doctrine. Mathematics has nothing to do with actual physical science. Science is based on the creation of *new principles* which mathematics had never been able to know.

So you make discoveries. You make scientific discoveries; you discover what Kepler did—he discovered the Solar System. Now we have a new development.

We have the—scientists today have discovered a higher order of life, of control over human life: the Galaxy, the galactic process.

And so, what we have to do, is go to the kind of thinking which is *not* statistical; get rid of the statisticians! They're idiots. And if you look at the thing, since 1890, there has been a consistent degeneration in practice of so-called science in the main, down, down, down, down, down, to the present nadir: doomsday.

Mankind Must Go Forward

What is required is we have to dump that junk, and go back to the principles of physical science, typified by those of Alexander Hamilton for the United States; and typified by the greatest scientists who actually lived in our lifetime, and there are a few of them. So that's what we have to do. We have to change the whole agenda, and that's not so difficult, because all you have to do is say, what're the phonies on your block? And you'll find a whole bunch of them, all ready, talking away like parrots! But the parrots won't talk, because they're ashamed of being in their presence.

So the point is, we do have the ability, as human beings, of rethinking what our mission is, and recognizing that some of the things we were taught to believe in were actually fake. And that's why we're having so many problems, including health problems.

Ascher: Lyn, if you could give us some summary remarks, perhaps you could summarize for us what should be the focus coming off the call here this evening.

LaRouche: Yeah, the point is we have to realize, as what started from Tony Papert, in his remarks which were done on the basis of my conception; that that's the way we have to go. We have to get rid of all this kind of practical shmactical kind of stuff, and realize that there are certain universal physical principles, efficient principles, which can be traced through the ups and downs of the development of progress, in terms of human development; we're now in a point where we have access to opportunities to discover things we have never dis-

NASA

"Mankind must reach levels of understanding, of the Solar System and beyond, beyond anything they've known before." Exemplary is this Mars Reconnaissance Orbiter, shown in artist's conception. The Orbiter went into operation in March 2006, and is now one of six active satellites over Mars, sending data back to Earth.

covered before. Like what the galactic issue is. That's a new phase for scientists in terms of practical today. And these are the kinds of things we must rely upon: Mankind must go forward! Mankind must reach levels of understanding, of the Solar System and beyond, beyond anything they've known before.

In great periods of history, mankind has always made, by some people at least, great contributions to mankind's knowledge of things that mankind had never known before! And that's the idea, to go where mankind has never gone before. And do it successfully. And that's the division. I mean, what does it mean, if you've got children, what do you want to give them? A sense of a future. What's a future? It means participating in where man is able to go, where mankind had never gone before.

And that's the whole name of the game. If you're trying to be practical, you ain't human.

Ascher: Thank you so much, Lyn. This is a tremendous discussion this evening. We'll be getting the recording out to everyone tomorrow, and that concludes our 10th Fireside Chat with Lyndon LaRouche. And so, goodnight, Lyn, and goodnight to everybody on the call.

LaRouche:: Thank you!

Cusa's Method of Creative Interruption

by William F. Wertz, Jr.

July 26—In a July 20 discussion, Lyndon LaRouche emphasized that society functions on the basis of abrupt interruptions which may change the entire direction of the action which had been going on before. In fact, voluntary human interruptions are the essential characteristic of a sane society. Mankind's natural tendency is a creative one, not a deductive one. The function of mankind is to make creative discoveries which define the future of mankind.

And that's what our problem is today: We've got to get rid of the mathematicians, the idea that you can use mathematics, which is only a deductive method; the deductive method will never give you a discovery as such. Mathematics is for lunatics. What kills us is the fact that people still believe in mathematics. Mathematics gives you a predetermined order. A true physical principle is never mathematical. The process of creating it is never mathematical.

Pragmatism is virtually enshrined as the national character of Americans. The repeated statements designed for every occasion: "Let's be practical;" "You have to go along to get along," the belief that you can't beat City Hall, that "they" will never let you do it, or never let it happen, are all reflections of the same empiricist-deductive mathematical mentality, which, unless rejected, ensures the doom of humanity.

The American poet and story-teller Edgar Allen Poe understood

"For just as God is the Creator of real entities and of natural forms, man is the creator of rational entities and artificial forms."—Nicolaus of Cusa. He's shown here on an early German book cover.

this well. In his short story "Mellonta Tauta," he exposed the fact that the oligarchy controls human beings to their own self-destruction, by convincing them that there are only "two possible roads for the attainment of Truth." He writes that long ago there lived a Turkish philosopher (or Hindoo) possibly called Aries Tottle. "This person introduced, or at all events propagated what was termed the deductive or a priori mode of investigation. He started with what he maintained to be axioms of 'self-evident truths,' and thence proceeded 'logically' to results. His greatest disciples were one Neuclid, and one Cant. Aries Tottle flourished supreme until the advent of one Hog ... who preached an entirely different system, which he called the a posteriori or inductive.... The savants now maintained that the Aristotelian and Baconian roads were the sole possible avenues to knowledge."

Poe described these two methods as "creeping" and "crawling," which he contrasted to the true nature of man, which is that the human soul loves nothing so well as to "soar." He then points to the method of Kepler as coherent with the true nature of man. He asks, do you think man could have attained to the idea of gravitation with these two methods? And how did Kepler discover this truth? Kepler admitted that his three laws were guessed at—that is to say, imagined.

The method of Kepler, as described by Poe, was introduced

to Kepler by Nicolaus of Cusa (or Cusanus), who used the method of "conjecture" or "hypothesis" developed by Plato to bring about a revolution in human history in the 1400s, a revolution which saved mankind from the otherwise certain doom of the Medieval Dark Ages in Europe under the Venetian system, which was an earlier version of the current British imperial system.

And it is only that method now, which can free mankind from the "practical" mental shackles of the Aristotelian and Baconian methods, which reduce him to a creeping or crawling animal preyed upon by the British Empire today.

The Promethean Method

The method of Cusanus, the method employed by Lyndon LaRouche, is also accurately referred to as the Promethean method.

In Plato's dialogue *Philebus*, Socrates says:

> There is a gift of the gods—so at least it seems evident to me—which they let fall from their abode, and it was through Prometheus, or one like him, that it reached mankind, together with a fire exceeding bright. The men of old, who were better than ourselves and dwelt nearer the gods, passed on this gift in the form of a saying. All things, so it ran, that are ever said to be, consist of a one and a many, and have in their nature a conjunction of limit and unlimitedness.

In the dialogue Plato first develops the conception of this conjunction of "the limit" and "unlimitedness," as a fixed limit which is imposed on unlimitedness. Such an Aristotelian conception only permits induction from the unlimited, and deduction from the fixed limit.

But what Socrates points out in the dialogue, is that another conjunction exists, besides the imposition of a limit on the family of the unlimited. That conjunction is an unlimited family of higher-order limits.

Plato then stresses that all things that come to be, should come to be because of some cause. Thus, he continues:

> The first, then, I call the unlimited, the second the limit, and the third, the being that has come to be by the mixture of these two; as for the fourth, I hope I shall not be at fault in calling it the cause of the mixture and of the coming-to-be.

Finally Plato stresses that there exists in the universe a "presiding cause of no mean power, which orders and regulates the years, the seasons and the months, and has every claim to the names of wisdom and reason, and that the human mind belongs to the family of this cause of all things."

In this dialogue, Plato thus develops that man, as Cusanus will later argue, is in the living image of the Creator, i.e. the human mind belongs to the family of the cause of all things, and that the nature of man's role in the universe is to bring into existence higher forms of existence, through the creation of an unlimited family of higher-order limits. Man is thus not defined by the imposition of a fixed limit on the unlimited, as defined by that fixed limit. In fact, such a notion is contrary to the very nature of man as a creator in the living image of the Creator.

The fact of the matter is that all progress in the physical universe and in human society, only occurs through the creative interruption of a fixed inductive/deductive system. It is for this reason that Lyndon LaRouche says that if you are practical, you are stupid, and responsible for your own destruction. The only thing worthy of the attention of a human being, is to concentrate on discovering and acting on those principles which make man the cause of the coming into being of a higher-order geometry, coherent with man's actual mission as the only creative immortal species.

The Circle Cannot Be Squared

The best way to access the contribution of Nicolaus of Cusa to this discussion, is by turning our attention to his refutation of the Aristotelian/Euclidean method of Archimedes, who argued that the circle can be squared.

In his "On the Quadrature of the Circle," (1450) (**Figure 1**) Nicolaus of Cusa proves that if one inscribes a polygon in a circle or circumscribes a circle with a polygon, the more sides one adds to the polygon, thus apparently approaching the circle, the more distant the polygon is from equality with the circle, by virtue of the unlimited multiplication of sides. The reason why the polygon can never become equal to the circle, is because, as Cusanus writes, "polygonal figures are not magnitudes of the same species as the circular figure."

> In respect to things which admit of a larger and smaller, one does not come to an absolute maximum in existence and potentiality. Namely, in comparison to the polygons, which admit of a

FIGURE 1
Quadrature of the Circle

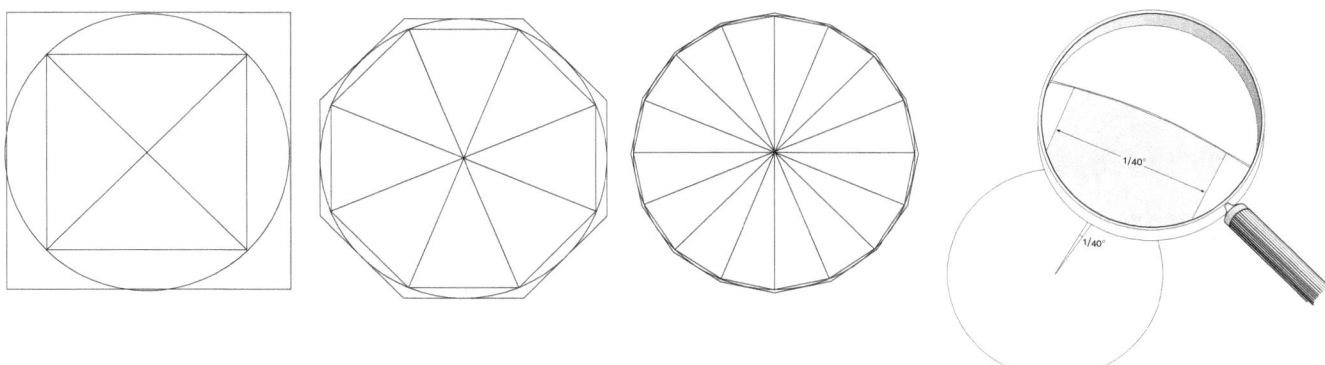

Nicholas of Cusa showed that Archimedes' attempt at "quadrature of the circle"—to approximate the value of pi—was ontologically incompetent. The first three drawings show the process of estimating the area of a square approximately equal to that of a given circle, as the average area of two regular polygons. In the last drawing, although the inscribed polygon of 216 may seem to closely approximate a circle in area, it actually contains a devastating paradox. There are slightly more than 182 angles of the inscribed polygon within each degree of circular arc.

larger and smaller, and thereby do not attain to the circle's area, the area of a circle is the absolute maximum, just as numerals do not attain the power of comprehension of unity, and multiplicities do not attain the power of the simple.

Cusanus goes on to say that some consider a square equal to the circle, if it is not larger or smaller than the circle by the smallest specifiable fraction of the square or the circle:

> If one apprehends the concept of equality in this way, then it is justly said that one can give an equal circumference to a given polygonal perimeter. However, if one apprehends the concept of equality, insofar as it relates to a magnitude, absolutely, without regard to rational fractions, then it is true that no precisely equal non-circular magnitude can be given for a circular magnitude.

In his most revolutionary work, *On Learned Ignorance* (Book I, Chapter 3), Cusanus also writes:

> For truth is not something more or something less, but is something indivisible. Whatever is not truth, cannot measure truth precisely. (By comparison, a non-circle [cannot measure] a circle, whose being is something indivisible.) Hence, the intellect, which is not truth, never

comprehends truth so precisely that truth cannot be comprehended infinitely more precisely. For the intellect is to truth as [an inscribed] polygon is to [the inscribing] circle. The more angles the inscribed polygon has, the more similar it is to the circle. However, even if the number of angles is increased ad infinitum, the polygon never becomes equal [to the circle]....

In another location in *On Learned Ignorance* Book III, Chapter 1, Cusanus writes:

> A square inscribed in a circle passes—with respect to its size—from being a square which is smaller than the circle to being larger than the circle, without ever arriving at its equal. And an angle of incidence increases from being lesser than a right [angle] to being greater [than a right angle] without the medium of equality.

This transition he describes as a "certain singularity."

As Lyndon LaRouche has pointed out, the Greeks had discovered incommensurability. They knew, for instance, that the diagonal of a square is incommensurate with the side. Archimedes believed that pi was similarly an irrational magnitude. But what Cusanus established, is that whereas the relationship of the diagonal to the side of the square is irrational, the relationship of the circle to the square is transcendental.

As LaRouche wrote in Appendix A to the "Truth About Temporal Eternity" (*Fidelio*, Vol. III, No. 2, of 1994):

> Cusanus recognized that circular action:
> (a) could not be defined ontologically within the implicitly axiomatic formalities of Greek mathematics, since the circular perimeter, the locus of that action, was an absolute mathematical discontinuity between the two transfinite series, inscribed and circumscribed, of polygonal processes.
> (b) Moreover, since those polygonal processes themselves were externally bounded by circular constructions, the axiomatic formalities implicitly underlying Archimedes' constructions could not access efficiently the ontological domain of circular action, but circular action could determine, and thus access efficiently the processes of the polygonal constructions' domain.
> (c) Therefore we must discard the implied set of axioms of Archimedes' use of the Euclidean domain, and replace those with the axiomatic quality (Platonic hypothesis of universal circular action [later, universal least action]).

Now the practical man or woman will ask: "What does this theoretical stuff have to do with me?" If you don't master its implications and act on the basis of it, it means that you are dead as a result of your own stupidity.

Take the example of the recent Encyclical released by the Vatican on Global Warming. Acceptance of this document will lead to your death as ineluctably as Jerry Brown's water-denial policy in California. Both are extensions of the genocidal policy of the Nazi-loving British royal family, which intends to reduce the world's population from seven billion to one billion by whatever means necessary, including thermonuclear war. If you accept the British Empire and its anti-scientific "Limits to Growth" genocidal policy, your death and that of six billion other human beings is deductively certain.

Riemann's Shock-Wave

The anti-deductive Promethean method developed by Cusanus was further developed by two German sci-

entists, Georg Cantor and Bernhard Riemann.

In his *Foundations of a General Theory of Manifolds* (1883) Cantor developed the conception of the transfinite. In doing so, he makes explicit reference to Plato's *Philebus* dialogue and to the work of Nicolaus of Cusa.

In one footnote to this work, Cantor says that he believes that his notion of the transfinite is related to that of the Platonic idea, as well as to that which Plato, in his *Philebus* dialogue, calls the mixture of the unlimited and the limit.

In a second footnote, he writes that "Plato's conception of the infinite is an entirely different one than that of Aristotle," and that "similarly, I find points of contact for my conceptions in the philosophy of Nicolaus Cusanus."

In *On Learned Ignorance* Book II, Cusanus indeed makes the point that since the Infinite Form is received only finitely, "every created thing is, as it were a finite infinity." And in Book III, Cusanus suggests that "species are like a number series which progresses sequentially."

In his habilitation dissertation, "On the Hypotheses which Lie at the Foundation of Geometry," Riemann develops the idea of a multiply extended manifold, i.e. an "endless series" of higher order manifolds. Riemann writes:

> If in the case of a notion whose specializations form a continuous manifold, one passes from a certain specialization in a definite way to another, the specializations passed over form a simply extended manifold, whose true character is that in it a continuous progress from a point is possible only in two directions, forwards or backwards. If one now supposes that his manifold in its turn passes over into another entirely different, and again in a definite way, namely so that each point passes over into a definite point of the other, then all the specializations so obtained form a doubly extended manifold. In a similar manner one obtains a triply extended manifold, if one imagines a doubly extended one passing over in a definite way to another entirely different; and it is easy to see how this construction may be continued.

Having thus rejected the Euclidean notion of geometry, Riemann concludes his habilitation paper by

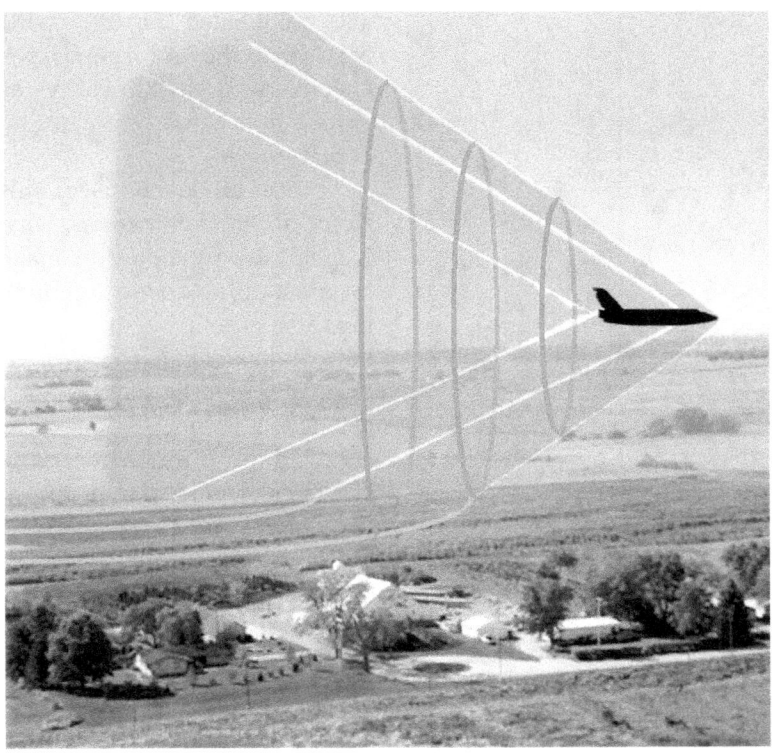

EIRNS

A jet plane crosses the "sound barrier," creating a shock wave popularly called a "sonic boom."

pointing out that one can only progress in mastering the laws of the physical universe by abandoning the false linear assumptions of mathematics. This conclusion, he says, "leads us into the domain of another science, that of physics, into which the object of today's proceedings does not allow us to enter."

In a later work "On the Propagation of Plane Waves of Finite Amplitude," Riemann, however, does precisely that,—he enters the domain of physics. In this paper, Riemann describes the generation of a hydrodynamic shock wave, in which a phase change is effected from an n-fold domain to an n+1-fold domain, which is entirely different. What Riemann describes in this paper, is perhaps best illustrated by the phenomenon, unknown during his lifetime, of an airplane exceeding the speed of sound. The speed of sound is a physical limit, which when it is exceeded generates a sonic boom. The creation of a sonic boom is a creative interruption of the subsonic linear geometry, and as such is a demonstration of principle.

In the 1500s, numerous Aristotelians, including Galileo Galilei, argued that Cusanus was wrong, and Archimedes was right. They insisted that the circle is a straight line in the infinitely small. Similarly in the 1890s, Lord Rayleigh, Bertrand Russell, and others insisted that Riemann's physics was absurd. Rayleigh, in particular, insisted that "sonic booms" could not exist.

Riemann refers to the hypotheses which underlie scientific progress as "Geistesmassen," or as Lyndon LaRouche terms them, "thought objects." Nicolaus of Cusa expresses this same idea in two of his writings. He refers to conjectures or hypotheses as "rational entities."

In *On Beryllus*, Cusanus writes:

For just as God is the Creator of real entities and of natural forms, man is the creator of rational entities and artificial forms. These are nothing other than similitudes of his intellect, just as the creatures of God are similitudes of the divine Intellect. Therefore man has intellect, which is a similitude of the divine Intellect, in creating. Therefore, he creates similitudes of the similitudes of the divine Intellect, so the extrinsic artificial figures are similitudes of intrinsic natural forms. Hence he measures his intellect through the power of his works and from this measures the divine Intellect, as the truth is measured through its image.

In *On Conjectures*, Cusanus makes a similar statement:

Conjectures must go forth from our minds as the real world does from the infinite divine Reason. For, since the human mind, the lofty similitude of God, participates, as far as possible in the fecundity of the creatrix nature, it exserts the rational from itself, as the image of omnipotent form, in the similitude of real entities.

In *On Conjectures*, Cusanus writes:

Man is indeed god, but not absolutely, since he is man; he is therefore a human god. Man is also the world, but not everything contractedly, since he is man. Man is therefore a microcosm or a human world. The region of humanity therefore embraces God and the whole world in its human potential.

Breaking Satanic Shackles

If you contrast this conception of man with that expressed in the recent encyclical of Pope Francis on the environment, *Laudato Si'*, it should be obvious to you that the current Pope has adopted, and is actively campaigning for, a conception which is actually Satanic, in that it denies man's true role, in the living image of the Creator, to do as Prometheus did. That is, to free mankind from the shackles imposed upon him by the Zeusian imperial system, today represented by the British Empire,— by mastering the laws of the universe, and by creating new forms of social organization.

The basis for achieving both of these objectives can be found in the "rational entities" generated by Nicolaus of Cusa in the 1400s.

"Prometheus carrying fire" by Jan Cossiers, 1600-1671.

First, it is man's destiny to be an instrument of the Creator exerting dominion not only over the earth, but over the universe, beginning with our galaxy.

In *On Learned Ignorance*, Book II, Cusanus devastated the Aristotelian conception which had been imposed on mankind since the time of Ptolemy,—the insistence that the earth is the immobile, fixed center of the universe around which the heavenly bodies orbit in circular orbits. Cusanus argued that in the created world, there can be no absolute maximum or minimum. Therefore "it is not possible for the world-machine to have, as a fixed and immovable center, either our perceptible earth or air or fire or any other thing."

On the same basis he argues that "the world does not have a fixed circumference." Therefore, he concludes, "just as the earth is not the center of the world, so the sphere of fixed stars is not its circumference." He continues: "It is evident that the earth is moved." Moreover, "neither the sun nor the moon nor the earth nor any sphere can by its motion describe a true circle, since none of these are moved about a fixed point." Cusanus

also concluded on the same basis that the universe is not characterized by linearity as argued by Euclid, but rather by curvature.

It was on the basis of this series of "thought objects," that Kepler was prompted to make his great discoveries concerning the solar system, beginning with his *Mysterium Cosmographicum*, in which he pays explicit tribute to Cusanus:

Now God decided that quantity should exist before all other things so that there should be a means of comparing a curved with a straight line. For in this one respect Nicolaus of Cusa and others seem to me divine, that they attached so much importance to the relationship between a straight and a curved line, and dared to liken a curve to God, a straight line to his creatures; and those who tried to compare the creator to his creatures, God to man, and divine judgment to human judgments did not perform much more valuable a service than those who tried to compare a curve with a straight line, a circle with a square.

The next time someone tells you to "be practical," and that you can't do anything to change things, think about how Nicolaus of Cusa's thought object in *On Learned Ignorance*, suddenly changed the entire direction of your existence as mediated by Kepler. And then think about the task of going beyond Kepler today, by mastering the laws of the Galaxy, so as to address among other things the question of how to solve the water crisis presently confronting California and other parts of the globe.

'Fire Within the Mind'

The second objective facing mankind today, which Nicolaus of Cusa uniquely addressed in the early 1430s, is defining the type of social organization we must develop on this planet to ensure that we fulfill our mission as human beings.

Nicolaus of Cusa addressed this question in 1433 in his work *De Concordantia Catholica*, which can be translated as "On Universal Concordance."

In the same July 20 discussion cited above, Lyndon LaRouche stated:

We're coming into a new era, for mankind. Everything is going to change. We're not going to have nations in the old sense any more, if we survive. Mankind is going to be more unified, if this works. It's going to be more unified than ever before. The separations of populations in a crucial way will disappear, gradually disappear.

Promethean man, as depicted by German Renaissance artist Albrecht Durer in his self-portrait, 1500.

Lyndon LaRouche had earlier expressed this idea in his *On the Science of Christian Economy* published in 1991. There he wrote:

What we must establish soon upon this planet, is not a utopia, but a Concordantia Catholica, a family of sovereign nation-state republics, each and all tolerating only one supranational authority, natural law, as the classical Christian humanists recognized it. Yet, it is not sufficient that each, as a sovereign republic, be subject passively to natural law. A right reading of that natural law reveals our obligation to co-sponsor certain regional and global cooperative ventures, in addition to our national affairs.

In *Concordantia Catholica*, Cusanus develops the notion expressed later in the U.S. Declaration of Independence, that government can only be established by election and by the consent of the governed. He states that the "common good only comes from the consent of all or of a majority.... All legitimate authority arises from elective concordance and free submission. There is in the people a divine seed by virtue of their common equal birth and the equal natural rights of all men, so that all authority—which comes from God as does man himself—is recognized as divine when it arises from the common consent of the subjects."

Nicolaus of Cusa also develops a higher conception capable of unifying humanity in the way discussed by Lyndon LaRouche, and now emerging among the BRICS nations.

The conception developed by Cusanus is that all human beings, and by implication all nations, must exist in "rational harmony with the Word," or the Logos or creative intellect. Cusanus argues that every concordance is made up of differences, but if all adhere to reason, then there is no opposition internally. Thus, he writes: "There is a concordance of differences among them. They enjoy together the good of one member, just as they suffer in common any evil, and they carry out their functions not only for themselves alone but rather for mutual benefit."

From what has been stated above, it should be clear that the gift of Prometheus is not fundamentally an external gift of fire. Such a gift is the result of a more fundamental gift. The fire Prometheus gave man was rather the self-consciousness of the fire within the mind to create necessary thought-objects, and the will to change the direction of humanity positively through the realization of those hypotheses. As Nicolaus of Cusa writes in *On Searching for God*: "Our intellectual spirit has the power of fire in itself."

When we exercise that power we are truly human. As Cusanus writes in Book III of *On Learned Ignorance*, when man has risen above sense perception and deductive thinking, to the level of creative intellect in harmony with the Logos, he has the power to command "even the evil spirits, and has power over nature and motion."

Isn't it time to give up our creep-crawly habits, and to truly soar like the human beings we were created to be?

The Coming Fall of the House of Windsor

by Helga Zepp-LaRouche

July 24—The revelations of the deep affinity between numerous members of the British royal family and Adolf Hitler—in light of the central role which British policy is playing both in the imposition of a brutal austerity policy on all of Europe, and in the confrontation course with Russia and China—ranks among the most important strategic developments of today. The quicker the House of Windsor lands in the rubbish heap of history, the better are the chances for reorganizing the totally bankrupt trans-Atlantic financial system, and avoiding a new—this time thermonuclear—world war.

In that context, the publication of a 17 second-long video, in which the seven or eight year old Elizabeth—later Queen Elizabeth II—is seen presenting a Hitler-salute, is only the tip of the iceberg. Since then, hundreds of articles have been circulated in the English and American press and on the Internet, which shed light on the open adulation of various members of the British Monarchy and British aristocracy for Hitler and the Nazis. The sympathies of Elizabeth's uncle, former King Edward VIII, who, after his abdication was called the Duke of Windsor, are well-known. More explosive is the role of Prince Philip, whose involvement, according to the British media, are to aired on July 30 on Channel Four of British TV, in a documentary called "The Plot to Make a King." In this, the close ties of Prince Philip to the Nazis are supposed to be uncovered, as well as the fact that his three sisters were all married to leading members of the National Socialist Party and the SS, and much more.

The *Times of Israel* on July 19 published an extensive interview with German-British historian Karina Urbach of the University of London, on the results of her research on this subject, which she has just published in a book with the title "Go-Betweens for Hitler." The book deals with the intense alliance between broad sections of the British Establishment and the Nazis, which alliance played a central role in British geopolitics between the world wars.

How did this material, which until now had previously been kept under absolute lock and key in the British archives, now become public in a way that can only be called a campaign? The background is, among other things, a kind of blood feud among the Windsors concerning the line of succession to Elizabeth II and Prince Philip, who are in the meantime considered too old to hold the British Empire together at a point in time when the trans-Atlantic financial system is on the edge of a crash, compared to which the collapse of Lehman Brother and AIG in 2008 was child's play. Part of the Windsor clan wants to skip over Prince Charles in the

A young Prince Philip, second from the right in the first row, marches in a funeral procession with SS friends in 1937. The picture, publicized in the 2006 book Royals and the Reich *by Jonathan Petropoulos, has been widely publicized in recent days.*

succession, and make William King; another faction is convinced that Great Britain can only save its relevance if it undergoes a fundamental restructuring of the whole Commonwealth. This second faction is apparently behind the revelations.

Environmentalist Fascists

But in the current strategic situation, the significance of the exposure of the Nazi sympathies of the British royals does not lie merely in hushed-up historical facts coming out, but in the meaning of this tradition for the political offensive which is using the so-called anthropogenic climate change as a pretext for the "decarbonization of the world economy"— an offensive which the British Monarchy is leading globally. Because if the goal of this climate-lobby, the goal of supporting the energy consumption of the entire world exclusively with so-called renewable energy sources—therefore excluding not only nuclear energy, but also all fossil fuel energy sources—were reached, then the number of people who could be sustained on Earth would be reduced from today's approximate seven billion, to one billion or less. Because there is a direct connection between the energy flux density used in the production process, which, with "renewable" energies is extremely low, and the potential population which can be supported.

Prince Philip is infamous for his statement that, in his opinion, the Earth is only suitable for one billion people, and he wrote in the foreword to his book *If I Were an Animal*, published in 1986, that he would like to be reincarnated as a deadly virus, in order to make a contribution to the reduction of the world's population. The same holds for the World Wildlife Fund and a whole number of other environmental organizations he founded, who, over the past decades, have sabotaged innumerable infrastructure projects in all parts of the world, and thereby have shortened the lives of millions of people.

At present a worldwide campaign is escalating, which would use the upcoming COP21 Climate Conference in December in Paris for the conclusive erection of a world dictatorship, through which the prescribed climate goals would strangle all development

ATP/Donald Stampfli

The Prince visits his own organization dedicated to population reduction, the World Wildlife Fund. Here he visits the WWF Switzerland in 1965.

of those formerly called developing countries. The fact that Hans Joachim Schellnhuber, who insists on being identified as "Commander of the British Empire," succeeded in writing his population-reducing theses on the "Great Transformation of Decarbonization of the World Economy" into the latest Encyclical of Pope Francis, *Laudato Si'*, represents a great catastrophe for the Catholic Church, of a sort that hasn't occurred since the Inquisition.

Prince Philip's adviser for religion and climate questions, Martin Palmer, who, in preparation for the December Conference, co-organized a so-called "Summit of Conscience" in Paris on July 21, in his role as general secretary of the "Alliance for Religion and the Environment" (ARC), attacked the "anthropocentric gospel" there. By this he means that religions such as Christianity, Judaism, and Islam have had difficulty understanding that man is simply not that important. He believes there must be a debate between members of these religions, in order to stamp out the idea that mankind represents something unique.

Here there comes to light the man-hating ideology which is the same as that of the Conservative Revolution, founded against the "ideas of 1789," and of the Nazis and the Green movement: that man is only a higher beast, and therefore human life should be no more sacrosanct than that of the animals; therefore, if required, the numbers of people could also be reduced—as the helots were in ancient Sparta, or the "useless eaters" under the Nazis, or even up to six billion people, who must be sacrificed to the goal of 'saving the climate." Armin Mohler, the former chairman of the Siemens Foundation, already wrote in his 1949 book *The Conservative Revolution* that the Conservative Revolution wanted to return to the pre-Christian Gaia-mythology, because the Christian image of man brought with it the cultural optimism, which made possible the modern development of mankind.

The sooner the whole historical truth about the British Empire leads to its well-deserved end, the better. The Indian opposition parliamentarian Shashi Tharoor performed a small, but important service July 24, in a brilliant speech at the University of Oxford on the crimes of this British Empire in its 200-year colonial domination of India. He pointed out that India's share of the world economy over this period was reduced from 23% to 4%, and that deliberately triggered famines costing 15 to 29 million Indians their lives.

For example, Winston Churchill deliberately ordered the removal of foodstuffs for the starving Bengali population, which cost four million Bengalis their lives in 1943. When conscience-stricken British officials alluded to the dimensions of the tragedy which his deci-

cc/Chatham House

Indian parliamentarian Shashi Tharoor's May 28 speech at the Oxford Union, detailing British genocide against India, has now gone viral. Here, Tharoor at Chatham House on June 2, 2015.

sion had caused, Churchill only answered: "Why hasn't Gandhi died yet?" The same Churchill in 1937 said before the House of Commons: "I did not suggest that, if I had to make a choice between communism and Nazism, I would choose communism."

The fall of the British monarchy would have a liberating effect for all Europe, but especially for Germany, because it would break the continuity of geopolitical manipulation and world wars which has persisted from the dismissal of Otto von Bismarck, deliberately arranged by the British manipulation, to the present day, and of which the tightening of austerity policy toward Greece after the visit of the Queen to Berlin, and the sanctions against Russia are only the latest examples.

But let it be said to the court lackies of the likes of Palmer and Schellnhuber: Mankind is a unique species, whose inviolable dignity lies in his creativity, which differentiates him from all animals. Mankind is the only creative species known so far, whose capability for discovering ever new and progressing universal principles, is capable of unlimited improvement, and which has explored the laws of the anti-entropically developing universe ever more successfully. And that applies in particular to the effects of the cycles of our Solar System and our Galaxy and their effect on the climate. Therefore the creativity of all mankind will undergo a gargantuan qualitative leap forward—after the downfall of the British monarchy.

The New Silk Road Becomes The World Land-Bridge

EIR Special Report

The New Silk Road Becomes The World Land-Bridge

The BRICS countries have a strategy to prevent war and economic catastrophe. It's time for the rest of the world to join!

This 374-page report is a road-map to the New World Economic Order that Lyndon and Helga LaRouche have championed for over 20 years. This path is currently being charted by the nations of the BRICS (Brazil, Russia, India, China, and South Africa), which are leading a dynamic of global optimism toward real economic development, complete with new credit institutions and major high-technology projects for uplifting all mankind.

Includes:

Introduction by Helga Zepp-LaRouche, "The New Silk Road Leads to the Future of Mankind!"

The metrics of progress, with emphasis on the scientific principles required for survival of mankind: nuclear power and desalination; the fusion power economy; solving the water crisis. Detailed maps show what has been accomplished and what has not, since Zepp-LaRouche first addressed a Beijing conference on the Eurasian Land-Bridge in 1996.

The three keystone nations: China, the core nation of the New Silk Road; Russia's mission in North Central Eurasia and the Arctic; India prepares to take on its legacy of leadership.

Other Regions: The potential contributions of Southwest, Central, and Southeast Asia; Australia as a driver for Pacific Development; Europe, the western pole of the New Silk Road; Africa—the Test for Global Progress; bringing the Western Hemisphere on board; the LaRouches' 40-year fight for international development.

www.ingramcontent.com/pod-product-compliance
Lightning Source LLC
Chambersburg PA
CBHW052041280526
45791CB00010B/3039